This volume, organizing and simplifying the thoughts of the "father of psychoanalysis," satisfies a longfelt need. It places all Freudiana within easy reach of professional and non-professional researchers alike.

Here the student can readily find Freud's exact statements on psychoanalytic questions, how he defined his original terms, as well as the changes and amplifications he made in his later writings. The quotations are presented under helpful subheadings and the sources from which they are taken identified.

FREUD

DICTIONARY OF PSYCHOANALYSIS

Edited by
NANDOR FODOR
and
FRANK GAYNOR

with a preface by
THEODOR REIK

A Fawcett Premier Book

FAWCETT PUBLICATIONS, INC., GREENWICH, CONN.
MEMBER OF AMERICAN BOOK PUBLISHERS COUNCIL, INC.

Preface

IT IS ONLY A FEW DECADES since Freud died in London. When I now read presentations of his work in books and articles, I am often reminded of a little story I heard as a boy in Vienna. The father of a peasant had died and the son, an Austrian Peter Simpleton, wished to possess a picture of the dear deceased man. The boy wandered to Vienna, found a well-known painter and described to the artist what the father looked like, giving full details of the shape of the face, the colors of hair and eyes a.s.o. The painter promised to deliver the picture. When the naive boy returned to the studio after a few weeks, he broke into sobs before the finished portrait and cried: "Poor father, how much you have changed in such a short time!" Reading many books and magazine articles of those last years that pretend to give a correct picture of Freud's ideas and teachings amazes us, who have known the great man: how much his thoughts have changed in such a short time!

Fortunately we have the possibility to study his work in the original. To remain within the simile, he has left us a magnificent self-portrait in those thirteen volumes of his writings.

The discussion about psychoanalysis among physicians and laymen (many of the first group belong also to the second) is rather increasing than diminishing. Everybody who has studied psychoanalysis thoroughly has, of course, the right to criticize the opinions of Freud. Nobody has the right to distort and misrepresent them. There ought to be a law!

This book will help to correct the abundant misunderstandings and misconceptions among the intelligent people interested in psychoanalysis. Presenting Freud's ideas in quotations from his own work, the editors have given a kind of dictionary which can secure authentic information on the most important topics of psychoanalysis to the student who is in doubt. Such a dictionary is, of course, not to be used as a textbook of psychoanalysis. It can rather be used to correct many textbooks, now printed.

It has become customary nowadays that the preface of a book should praise it in glowing terms, announce its publication with fanfare. (It is a custom more honour'd in the breach than the observance.) It is, it seems to me, sufficient to recommend its value to the intelligent reader. The editors of this book know, I am sure, that it is as imperfect as other scientific endeavors of this kind. They are willing, no, more than this, they are eager to augment and correct it, to fill gaps in later editions which will become necessary because the merits of such a work will soon be recognized by the students of psychoanalysis.

Greek mythology tells the story of the Augean stable wherein three thousand oxen were kept and which remained uncleaned for thirty years. The misconceptions and distortions, the falsifications and misrepresentations to which psychoanalysis was subjected in its popularization threaten to transform the magnificent house that Freud built into a stable similar to that of King Augeas. It too was not cleaned for thirty years and was, alas, frequented by more than 3000 oxen in this time. To clean it is a task compared with which Hercules had an easy job. The editors of this book have attempted to sweep at least a corner of this wide hall. Their endeavor is worthy of sincere acknowledgment.

THEODOR REIK

Introduction

THIS IS A BOOK that should satisfy a longfelt need. Freud's writings comprise a small library. To know how the founder of psychoanalysis defined his original terms, how he changed or amplified them in his later writings; to have his exact statements at hand on all possible psychoanalytic questions will be of considerable assistance to students and practitioners alike. Some analysts, known as specialists in Freudian quotations, have been receiving constant requests to supply references to those who sorely needed them. This book will safeguard them from the penalty of specialization, and will place all Freudiana within easy reach of professional and non-professional researchers.

Every possible care was taken to preserve the context of the original definitions and to present, in sub-headings, the varieties of application. The books from which the quotations are taken are easy to identify. Page references within the chapters have been avoided owing to the confusion which the plurality of editions would create.

THE EDITORS

A

ABASIA—See *Walking*.

ABSTINENCE, SEXUAL—In considering the question of abstinence, far too little distinction is made between two forms of it, namely, abstention from any kind of sexual activity at all, and abstention from heterosexual intercourse. *CSMN*

ACCIDENTAL ACTIONS—See *Chance Actions*.

ADAPTABILITY, CULTURAL—A man's personal capacity for transformation of the egoistic impulses under the influence of the erotic. *TTWD*

AFFECTIVITY—Affectivity manifests itself essentially in motor (*i.e.* secretory and circulatory) discharge resulting in an (internal) alteration of the subject's own body without reference to the outer world. *Ucs*

AGGRESSION—The tendency to aggression is an innate, independent, instinctual disposition in man. *C & D—ch. 6*

When the superego begins to be formed, considerable amounts of the aggressive instinct become fixated within the ego and operate there in a self-destructive fashion.
OoPA—ch. 2

The holding back of aggressiveness is in general unhealthy and leads to illness. *OoPA—ch. 2*

AGORAPHOBIA—The sufferer from agoraphobia imposes a restriction upon his ego in order to escape an instinctual danger. The instinctual danger in question is the temptation to yield to his erotic desires; and to yield to them would be to reincarnate once again, as in childhood, the specter of the danger of castration or of an analogous danger. As an example I may refer to the case of a young man who became agoraphobic because he was afraid of yielding to the allurements of prostitutes and of acquiring syphilis as a punishment. The symptomatology of agoraphobia is complicated by the fact that the ego is not content with renouncing something; in addition to this, it takes steps to deprive the situation of its danger. This additional

9

measure is usually a regression to childhood (in extreme cases, to the uterus, to a period when one was protected against the dangers which threaten today); the regression constitutes the condition under which the renunciation need not be made. Thus the agoraphobic may go on the street provided that, like a small child, he is accompanied by a person in whom he has full confidence. A similar caution may also permit him to go out alone, provided that he does not go more than a certain distance away from home, that he does not enter localities which he does not know well and where the people do not know him. In the choice of these specifications there becomes manifest the influence of the infantile motives which govern him.   *PoA—ch. 7*

AMBITION—A . . . connection is to be found between ambition and urethral erotism.   *NILP—ch. 4*

AMBIVALENCE—This form of the sexual organization can already maintain itself throughout life and draws to itself a large part of sexual activity. The dominance of sadism and the rôle of the cloaca of the anal zone stamps it with an exquisitely archaic impression. As another characteristic belonging to it, we can mention the fact that the contrasting pair of impulses are developed in almost the same manner, a situation which was happily designated by Bleuler by the term *ambivalence*.
TCTS II

AMNESIA

   Amnesia, Hysterical—In hysteria it is possible for a traumatic impression to become subjected to amnesia. [Cf. also *Amnesia, Infantile and Hysterical; Isolation.*]
PoA—ch. 6

   Amnesia, Infantile—The peculiar amnesia which veils from most people (not from all) the first years of their childhood, usually the first six or eight years.   *TCTS II*

With few exceptions, the events of the early period of sexuality fall a victim to *infantile amnesia*.   *OoPA—ch. 3*

I believe we accept too indifferently the fact of *infantile amnesia*—that is, the failure of memory for the first years of our lives—and fail to find in it a strange riddle.
PEL—ch. 4

The period of *infantile amnesia* coincides with this early blossoming of sexuality.   *M & M—Part III, Section I*

The period of infantile amnesia is often interrupted by isolated fragmentary memories, the so-called "screen-memories."
                                        M & M—Part III, Section I

Amnesia, Hysterical and Infantile, Compared—We shall not, however, hesitate to assert that the existence of the infantile amnesia gives us a new point of comparison between the psychic states of the child and those of the psychoneurotic. We have already encountered another point of comparison when confronted by the fact that the sexuality of the psychoneurotic preserves the infantile character or has returned to it. May there not be an ultimate connection between the infantile and the hysterical amnesias?

The connection between infantile and hysterical amnesias is really more than a mere play of wit. Hysterical amnesia which serves the repression can only be explained by the fact that the individual already possesses a sum of memories which were withdrawn from conscious disposal and which by associative connection now seize that which is acted upon by the repelling forces of the repression emanating from consciousness. We may say that without infantile amnesia there would be no hysterical amnesia.

I therefore believe that the infantile amnesia which causes the individual to look upon his childhood as if it were a *prehistoric* time and conceals from him the beginning of his own sexual life—that this amnesia is responsible for the fact that one does not usually attribute any value to the infantile period in the development of the sexual life. One single observer cannot fill the gap which has been thus produced in our knowledge.
                                        TCTS II

ANAL CHARACTER—In the course of studies of the pregenital phases of the libido, we have gleaned some new pieces of information about the formation of character. We have been made aware of a triad of characteristics which are almost always to be found together: orderliness, parsimoniousness and obstinacy, and we have concluded from the analysis of persons possessing them that these characteristics proceed from the dissipation of their anal-erotism and its employment in other ways. Where this remarkable combination is to be found, therefore, we speak of an *'anal character,'* and in a sense contrast it with unmodified anal-erotism.   *NILP—ch. 4*

ANALYSIS [cf. also PSYCHOANALYSIS]—When in analysis we render the ego assistance enabling it to undo its repressions, the ego regains its power over the repressed id and can so steer the course of the instinctual impulses as if the old danger situation no longer existed. What we achieve in this way is in complete harmony with what we accomplish in other spheres of medical activity. As a rule our treatment has to be satisfied with bringing about more rapidly, more certainly and with less trouble the satisfactory outcome which under favorable conditions would have resulted spontaneously.

PoA—ch. 10

Analysis is built on complete frankness.   *QLA—ch. 4*

Analysis of Children—Naturally one has to make extensive alterations in the technique of treatment which has been developed for adults when one is dealing with children. The child is, psychologically, a different thing from the adult; it does not yet possess a super-ego, it cannot make much use of the method of free association, and transference plays a different part with it, since its real parents are still there. The internal resistances, against which we have to fight in the case of adults, are in the case of children for the most part replaced by external difficulties.   *NILP—ch. 6*

Analysis, Fundamental Rule of—We impose upon him [the neurotic] the *fundamental rule* of analysis, which is henceforward to govern his behavior to us. He must tell us not only what he can say intentionally and willingly, what will give him relief like a confession, but everything else besides that his self-observation presents him with—everything that comes into his head, even if it is *disagreeable* to say it, even if it seems *unimportant* or positively *meaningless*.

OoPA—ch. 6

Analysis, Technique of—An analysis must go back to the patient's early childhood, because it was then, while the Ego was weak, that the decisive repressions occurred.

QLA—ch. 4

A correct reconstruction of such forgotten childhood experiences always has great therapeutic effects, whether it can also be confirmed from outside sources or not.   *QLA—ch. 4*

We induce the thus enfeebled [neurotic] ego to take part in the purely intellectual work of interpretation, which aims at provisionally filling the gaps in his mental resources, and to transfer to us the authority of his superego; we stimulate his ego to take up the struggle over each individual demand made by the id and to defeat the resistances which arise in connection with it. At the same time, we restore order in his ego, by detecting the material and impulses which have forced their way in from the unconscious, and expose them to criticism by tracing them back to their origin.   *OoPA—ch. 6*

The analyst never encourages the patient into the sexual field, he does not say in advance, "We must deal with the intimacies of your sexual life"! He lets him begin his communications where he likes, waiting quietly until he himself touches on sexual matters.   *QLA—ch. 4*

Analysis, dreams in the—The analyst links up the communication which he has received in the form of a dream with the patient's other communications and proceeds with the analysis.   *NILP—ch. 1*

Analysis, technique of—In civilian life illness may be used as a protection—to palliate incapacity at work or among competitors, or in family life as a means to force sacrifices and demonstrations of affection from others, or impose one's will upon them. All this is comparatively on the surface, and we put it all together under the heading "advantage gained by illness"; the only remarkable thing is that the patient—his Ego—knows nothing of the whole connection of such motives with his resulting behavior. One combats the influence of these impulses by forcing the Ego to accept this knowledge.
                    QLA—ch. 5

ANALYST—No one should practice analysis who has not qualified himself by a proper training. Whether the person is a doctor or not seems to me of altogether minor importance. [Cf. *Lay Analyst*.]   *QLA—ch. 5*

Analyst, personal influence of—Such an influence does exist, and plays a big part in the analysis. We do not employ this personal influence—the "suggestive" element—to suppress the symptoms from which the patient suffers, as is done in hypnotic suggestion. Further, it would be a mistake to think that this element bears the brunt and provides the main furtherance in the treatment. At first, yes; but later it stands in the way of our analytical purposes, and forces us to take most extensive countermeasures.   *QLA—ch. 1*

The neurotic sets himself to the work because he believes in the analyst, and he believes in him because he begins to entertain certain feelings towards him. The attitude is, in fact— to put it bluntly—a kind of falling in love. The patient *repeats,* in the form of falling in love with the analyst, psychical experiences which he underwent before; he has *transferred* to the analyst psychical attitudes which lay ready within him, and which were intimately linked with the inception of his neurosis. He repeats, too, his onetime defense reactions before our eyes, and wants nothing so much as to repeat all the vicissitudes of that forgotten period in his relations with the analyst. So what he is showing us is the very core of his most private life; *he is palpably reproducing it, as though it were all happening in the present, instead of remembering it.* With this, the riddle of transference-love is solved, and with the very help of the new situation, which seemed so threatening, the analysis can make progress. [Cf. *Transference in Analysis.*] *QLA—ch. 5*

ANALYTIC SITUATION—The analytical physician and the weakened ego of the patient, basing themselves upon the real external world, are to combine against the enemies, the instinctual demands of the id, and the moral demands of the superego. We form a pact with each other. The patient's sick ego promises us the most complete candor, promises, that is, to put at our disposal all of the material which his self-perception provides; we, on the other hand, assure him of the strictest discretion and put at his service our experience in interpreting material that has been influenced by the unconscious. Our knowledge shall compensate for his ignorance and shall give his ego once more mastery over the lost provinces of his mental life. This pact constitutes the analytic situation.

OoPA—ch. 6

ANIMISM AND ANIMATISM—Animism in the narrower sense is the theory of psychic concepts, and in the wider sense, of spiritual beings in general. Animatism, the animation theory of seemingly inanimate nature, is a further subdivision which also includes animatism and animism. The name animism, formerly applied to a definite philosophic system, seems to have acquired its present meaning through E. B. Taylor.

T & T—ch. 3

ANOREXIA—The most frequent disturbance of the nutritive function is anorexia through withdrawal of libido.

PoA—ch. 1

ANTICATHEXIS—A process which maintains the repression in the first case and, in the second, ensures its being established and continued by means of which the system Pcs guards itself against the intrusion of the unconscious idea. *Ucs*

Reaction formation in the ego, through an intensification of the attitude which is the antithesis of the instinctual tendency to be repressed (pity, conscientiousness, cleanliness). It is much more difficult to demonstrate anticathexis in hysteria, where, theoretically, it is just as indispensable. *PoA—ch. 11*

See also: ego-resistance.

Anticathexis, External and Internal—The contrast in the direction of the anticathexis as between hysteria and phobia on the one hand and compulsion neurosis on the other appears to be of importance, even though this antithesis is not an absolute one. It leads us to suppose that a rather intimate connection exists between repression and external anticathexis, as well as between regression and internal anticathexis (ego-alteration through reaction formation). *PoA—ch. 11*

Anticathexis in Hysteria—The hysterical type of anticathexis is predominantly directed outwards, against the dangerous perception; it takes the form of a special watchfulness which, through restrictions imposed upon the ego, avoids situations in which such a perception would inevitably occur, and which effects the withdrawal of attention from the perception if this has actually occurred. *PoA—ch. 11*

Anticathexis in Phobias—Even more strikingly than in hysteria is this technique of anticathexis displayed in the phobias, the interest of which is concentrated upon effecting a further and further removal of the possibility of experiencing the dreaded perception. *PoA—ch. 11*

ANXIETY—Anxiety is in the first place something felt. We call it an affective state, although we are equally ignorant of what an affect is. As a feeling it is of most obviously unpleasurable character, but this is not by any means a complete description of its quality; not every state of unpleasure may we call anxiety.

The analysis of the anxiety state gives us as its attributes: (1) a specific unpleasurable quality, (2) efferent or discharge phenomena, and (3) the perception of these. *PoA—ch. 8*

Anxiety is a specific state of unpleasure accompanied by motor discharge along definite pathways. *PoA—ch. 8*

Anxiety is the reaction to the danger of object loss.
PoA—ch. 11

The psychology of the neuroses taught us that when wish

feelings undergo repression their libido becomes transformed
into anxiety.   *T & T—ch. 2*

When the ego is forced to acknowledge its weakness, it
breaks out into anxiety: reality anxiety in face of the external
world, normal anxiety in face of the super-ego, and neurotic
anxiety in face of the strength of the passions in the id.

NILP—ch. 3

The ego withdraws (preconscious) cathexis from the instinct representative which is to be repressed and utilizes it in
the release of unpleasure (anxiety).   *PoA—ch. 2*

We have no reason to ascribe any expression of anxiety to
the superego. Anxiety is an affective state which can of course
be experienced only by the ego. The id cannot be afraid, as
the ego can; it is not an organization, and cannot estimate
situations of danger.   *PoA—ch. 8*

Anxiety is after all only a perception—of possibilities of
anxiety.   *C & D—ch. 8*

[Cf. also *Birth and Anxiety; Dread.*]

Anxiety as an Affective Condition—As an affective condition, anxiety is the reproduction of an old danger-threatening
event; anxiety serves the purposes of self-preservation as being
a signal of the presence of a new danger; it arises from libido
that has become unusable for some reason or other, including
the process of repression; it is replaced by symptom-formation,
and is thus, as it were, physically bound.   *NILP—ch. 4*

Anxiety in Dreams—See *Dreams, Anxiety.*

Anxiety and Expectation—Anxiety is undeniably related
to expectation; one feels anxiety lest something occur.

PoA—ch. 11

Anxiety in Hysteria and Other Neuroses—. . . it is to
the process of repression that we attribute the appearance of
anxiety in hysteria and other neuroses.   *NILP—ch. 4*

Anxiety, Instinctual—It may also be quite often the case
that in a danger situation which is correctly assessed as such
a modicum of instinctual anxiety is superadded to the reality
anxiety. The instinctual demand from the gratification of
which the ego shrinks back would then be the masochistic
one, the destructive impulse turned against the subject's own
person. Perhaps this superadded element explains the case of
the anxiety reaction becoming excessive and inexpedient,

paralyzing. The fear of high places might have this origin; its hidden feminine significance is suggestive of masochism.

PoA—ch. 11

Anxiety, Neurotic—Neurotic anxiety is anxiety in regard to a danger which we do not know. *PoA—ch. 11*

In a little essay on *Anxiety Neurosis,* written in 1895, I maintain that neurotic anxiety has its origin in the sexual life, and corresponds to a libido which has been deflected from its object and has found no employment. The accuracy of this formula has since then been demonstrated with ever-increasing certainty. From it we may deduce the doctrine that anxiety-dreams are dreams of sexual content, and that the libido appertaining to this content has been transformed into anxiety.

IoD—ch. 4

Anxiety, Object of—Let us call such a [danger] situation, in which the efforts of the pleasure-principle come to nothing, a "traumatic" factor; in that way, by following the series, neurotic anxiety—objective anxiety—danger-situation, we can arrive at a simple formula: what is feared, the object of the anxiety, is always the emergence of a traumatic factor, which cannot be dealt with in accordance with the norms of the pleasure-principle. *NILP—ch. 4*

Anxiety and Repression—It may still be correct to say that in repression anxiety is created out of the libidinal cathexis of instinctual impulses. *PoA—ch. 4*

Anxiety, Reproduction of—Anxiety arose as a response to a situation of *danger;* it will be regularly reproduced thenceforward whenever such a situation recurs. *PoA—ch. 8*

Anxiety, Sexual Practices and—I found that certain sexual practices, such as coitus interruptus, frustrated excitement, enforced abstinence, give rise to outbreaks of anxiety and a general predisposition to anxiety—which may be induced whenever, therefore, sexual excitation is inhibited, frustrated or diverted in the course of its discharge in gratification. *PoA—ch. 4*

Anxiety, Signal of—An increase in unpleasure which is expected and foreseen is met by a *signal of anxiety;* the occasion of this increase, whether it threatens from without or within, is called a *danger.* *OoPa—ch. 1*

Anxiety, True (Real) and Neurotic—A real danger is a danger which we know, a true anxiety the anxiety in regard to such a known danger. Neurotic anxiety is anxiety in regard to a danger which we do not know. . . . There are cases in which the attributes of true and of neurotic anxiety are inter-mingled. The danger is known and of the real type, but the anxiety in regard to it is disproportionately great, greater than in our judgment it ought to be. It is by this excess that the neurotic element stands revealed.   *PoA—ch. 11*

ANXIETY-DREAM—See *Dream, Anxiety*.

ANXIETY-HYSTERIA—See *Phobia*.

ANXIETY-NEUROSIS—Hereditary disposition is the most important determinant of anxiety-neurosis, but not an *indispensable* one, since it is lacking in a series of borderline cases. [Cf. *Anxiety, neurotic; Neurasthenia*.]   *RCA-N*

ANXIETY-PREPAREDNESS—In our analysis of objective anxiety we explained it as a condition of increased sensory attention and motor tension, which we called '*anxiety-preparedness*.' Out of this the anxiety-reaction arises.   *NILP—ch. 4*

ANXIETY-REACTION—The anxiety-reaction may run one of two courses. Either the *anxiety-development*, the repetition of the old traumatic experience, is restricted to a signal, in which case the rest of the reaction can adapt itself to the new situation of danger, whether by flight or defence; or the old experience gets the upper hand, and the whole reaction exhausts itself in anxiety-development, in which case the affective state is paralysing and unadapted to the present situation.
     NILP—ch. 4

ANXIOUS EXPECTATION—See: *Expectation, Anxious*.

APPREHENSION—Apprehension denotes a certain condition as of expectation of danger and preparation for it, even though it be an unknown one.   *BPP—ch. 2*

ARCHAIC HERITAGE IN MENTAL LIFE—See *Racial Memory*.

ART—Incomplete and dim memories of the past, which we call tradition, are a great incentive to the artist, for he is free to fill in the gaps in the memories according to the behests of his imagination and to form after his own purpose the image of the time he has undertaken to reproduce.
     M & M—Part III, Section I

As artistic talent and productive ability are intimately connected with sublimation, we have to admit also that the nature of artistic attainment is psychoanalytically inaccessible to us.
LDV—ch. 6

ASSOCIATIONS—Whenever one psychic element is connected with another by an obnoxious and superficial association, there exists also a correct and more profound connection between the two, which succumbs to the resistance of the censorship.
IoD—ch. 7

Associations in Dream Interpretation—Although in dream interpretation we are in general and predominantly dependent on the associations of the dreamer, nevertheless we treat certain elements of the content quite independently—mainly because we have to, because as a rule, associations refuse to come.
NILP—ch. 1

The associations to the dream are not the latent dream-thoughts. They are contained, but not completely contained, in the associations.
NILP—ch. 1

ATTENTION—A special function which has periodically to search the outer world, in order that its data might be already familiar if an urgent inner need should arise.
FPMF

AUTOEROTISM—The most striking character of this sexual activity is that the impulse is not directed to other persons but that the child gratifies himself on his own body; to use the happy term invented by Havelock Ellis, we will say that he is *autoerotic.*
TCTS II

B

BEAUTY—Beauty is an instance which plainly shows that culture is not simply utilitarian in its aims, for the lack of beauty is a thing we cannot tolerate in civilization.

C & D—ch. 3

BED-WETTING—We are inclined to adopt the simple generalization that continued bed-wetting is a result of masturbation and that its suppression is regarded by boys as an inhibition of their genital activity, that is, as having the meaning of a threat of castration; but whether we are always right in supposing this remains to be seen.

AnDS

BEHEADING—Certain patients suffering from obsessions treat being beheaded as a substitute for being castrated.

C-S & S

BIOLOGY—The impulses and their transformations are the last things psychoanalysis can discern. Henceforth it leaves the stage to biological investigation. . . . Biological investigation of our time endeavors to explain the chief traits of the organic constitution of a person through the fusion of male and female predispositions in the material sense.

LDV—ch. 6

BIRTH—The first anxiety experience, of the human being at least, is birth; and this means, objectively, separation from the mother, and could be likened to a castration of the mother (in accordance with the equation: child = penis).

PoA—ch. 7

Birth can hardly in itself be regarded as an injury, although it may involve a risk of injury. The fundamental thing about birth, as about every danger-situation, is that it evokes in mental experience a condition of tense excitation, which is felt as pain, and which cannot be mastered by discharge.

NILP—ch. 4

Birth and Anxiety—I am forced to the conclusion that the earliest phobias of childhood do not permit of being

20

directly traced to the impression made upon the child by the act of birth, and that they have thus far, in fact, defied all explanation. A certain predisposition to anxiety on the part of the infant is indubitable. *PoA—ch. 8*

The danger attending birth has still no psychic content. For certainly we cannot imagine as existing in the fœtus anything which in the least approaches any sort of knowledge of the possibility of death as an outcome. The fœtus can be aware of nothing beyond a gross disturbance in the economy of its narcissistic libido. Large amounts of excitation press upon it, giving rise to novel sensations of unpleasure; numerous organs enforce increased cathexes in their behalf, as it were a prelude to the object-cathexis soon to be initiated. *PoA—ch. 8*

I consider it inadmissible to assume that in every outbreak of anxiety something occurs in the psyche which is analogous to a reproduction of the birth situation. *PoA—ch. 2*

BISEXUALITY—Man, too, is an animal with an unmistakably bisexual disposition. The individual represents a fusion of two symmetrical halves, of which, according to many authorities, one is purely male, the other female. *C & D—ch. 4*

Parts of the male sexual apparatus are also to be found in the body of the female, although in a rudimentary condition, and *vice versa*. Science sees in this phenomenon an indication of *bi-sexuality*, as though the individual were neither man nor woman, but both at the same time, only rather more the one than the other. *NILP—ch. 5*

For the purpose of distinguishing between male and female in mental life we assert an equivalence which is clearly insufficient, empirical and conventional: we call everything that is powerful and active "male" and everything that is weak and passive "female." *OoPA—ch. 7*

BODY—The body itself, and above all its surface, is a place from which both external and internal perceptions may spring. *E & I—ch. 2*

BRAID-SNIPPERS—The "braid-snippers," without knowing it, play the part of persons who perform the act of castration on the female genital. *LDV—ch. 3*

C

CASTRATION ANXIETY (FEAR, COMPLEX)—A male child commonly suffers from anxiety lest his father rob him of his male member; and so castration anxiety is one of the strongest influences on the development of his character, and decisive for his sexual tendencies later. *QLA—ch. 4*

Before the child came under the domination of the castration complex, at the time when he still held the woman at her full value, he began to manifest an intensive desire to look, as an erotic activity of his impulse. He wished to see the genitals of other persons, originally probably because he wished to compare them with his own. The erotic attraction which emanated from the person of his mother soon reached its height in the longing to see her genital, which he believed to be a penis. With the cognition acquired only later that the woman has no penis, this longing often becomes transformed into its opposite and gives place to disgust, which in the years of puberty may become the cause of psychic impotence, of misogyny and of lasting homosexuality. But the fixation on the once so vividly desired object, the penis of the woman, leaves ineradicable traces in the psychic life of the child, which has gone through that fragment of infantile sexual investigation with particular thoroughness. The fetish-like reverence for the feminine foot and shoe seems to take the foot only as a substitutive symbol for the once revered and since then missed member of the woman. The "braid-snippers," without knowing it, play the part of persons who perform the act of castration on the female genital. *LDV—ch. 3*

Castration Motive in the Oedipus Complex—Castration has a place, too, in the Œdipus legend, for the blinding with which Œdipus punished himself after the discovery of his crime is, by the evidence of dreams, a symbolic substitute for castration. *OoPA—ch. 7*

Castration Anxiety in Phobias—The fear in zoöphobia is castration anxiety on the part of the ego, that in agoraphobia (though this has been less thoroughly studied) seems to be a fear of temptation, which must certainly be related genetically to castration anxiety.   *PoA*—ch. 4

Castration Complex in Women—Fear of castration is naturally not the only motive for repression; to start with, it has no place in the psychology of women; they have, of course, a castration-complex, but they cannot have any fear of castration. In its place, for the other sex, is found fear of the loss of love, obviously a continuation of the fear of the infant at the breast when it misses its mother.   *NILP*—ch. 4

See *Penis-Envy; Œdipus Complex.*

CATHECT, CATHEXIS—The words "cathexis" and "to cathect" are used as renderings of the German *"Besetzung"* and *"besetzen."* These are the terms with which Freud expresses the idea of physical energy being lodged in or attaching itself to mental structures or processes, somewhat on the analogy of an electric charge.   *OoPA*—ch. 2

Cathexis, from the Greek *cathexo,* I occupy; the term refers to a sum of psychic energy, which occupies or invests objects or some particular channels.   *WRU*—ch. V

CHANCE ACTIONS—Chance actions differ from erroneously carried-out actions only in that they disdain the support of a conscious intention and really need no pretext. They appear independently and are accepted because one does not credit them with any aim or purpose. We execute them "without thinking anything of them," "by mere chance," "just to keep the hands busy," and we feel confident that such information will be quite sufficient should one inquire as to their significance. In order to enjoy the advantage of this exceptional position, these actions which no longer claim awkwardness as an excuse must fulfill certain conditions: they must not be striking, and their effects must be insignificant. (See also *Symptomatic and Chance Actions.*)   *PEL*—ch. 9

That accidental actions are really intentional will find no greater credence in any other sphere than in sexual activity, where the border between the intention and accident hardly seems discernible. . . . An apparently clumsy movement may be utilized in a most refined way for sexual purposes.   *PEL*—ch. 8

CHARACTER—What we call the *character* of the person is built up to a large extent from the material of sexual excitations; it is composed of impulses fixed since infancy and won through sublimation, and of such structures as are destined to suppress effectually those perverse feelings which are recognized as useless.   *TCTS III*

CHILD—A more searching investigation into the psychic life of the child teaches us, of course, that sexual motives, in infantile forms, play a very considerable part, which has been too long overlooked, in the psychic activity of the child. This permits us to doubt to some extent the happiness of the child, as imagined later by adults.   *IoD—ch. 3*

The child is long before puberty a being capable of mature love, lacking only the ability for reproduction.   *SECh*

See also *Childhood; Lies, Children's; Sexuality in Childhood.*

Girls—A comparison with what happens in the case of the boy shows us that the development of the little girl into a normal woman is more difficult and more complicated.
                                                     NILP—ch. 5

The little girl is as a rule less aggressive, less defiant, and less self-sufficient; she seems to have a greater need for affection to be shown her, and therefore to be more dependent and docile. . . . One gets the impression, too, that the little girl is more intelligent and more lively than the boy of the same age; she is more inclined to meet the external world half way, and, at the same time, she makes stronger object-cathexes.
                                                     NILP—ch. 4

Children, Amorality of—Small children are notoriously amoral. They have no internal inhibitions against their pleasure-seeking impulses.   *NILP—ch. 3*

Child, Attitude to Brothers and Sisters—A child is absolutely egotistical; he feels his wants acutely, and strives remorselessly to satisfy them, especially against his competitors, other children, and first of all against his brothers and sisters. . . . I seriously declare it as my opinion that a child is able to estimate the disadvantages which he has to expect on account of a new-comer.   *IoD—ch. 5*

Child, Development of—Both sexes seem to pass through the early phases of libidinal development in the same way. . . .

With the onset of the phallic phase the difference between the sexes becomes much less important than their similarities. (Cf. *Pregenital Phases*.)   *NILP—ch. 5*

Child and the Genitals—When the male child first directs his curiosity to the riddle of the sexual life, he is dominated by the interest for his own genitals. He finds this part of the body too valuable and too important to believe that it would be missing in other persons to whom he feels such a resemblance. As he cannot divine that there is still another equally valuable type of genital formation he must grasp the assumption that all persons, also women, possess such a member as he. This preconception is so firm in the youthful investigator that it is not destroyed even by the first observation of the genitals in little girls.   *LDV—ch. 3*

CHILD-PENIS WISH—See *Penis-Envy*.

CHILD PSYCHOLOGY—Child pschology, in my opinion, is destined to render the same services to the psychology of adults as a study of the structure or development of the lower animals renders to the investigation of the structure of the higher orders of animals.   *IoD—ch. 3*

CHILDHOOD

Childhood Experiences—The psychoanalyses of individuals have taught us that their earliest impressions, received at a time when they were hardly able to talk, manifest themselves later in an obsessive fashion, although those impressions themselves are not consciously remembered.

M & M—Part III, Section II

The experience of the first five years of childhood exerts a decisive influence on our life, one which later events oppose in vain. . . . The strongest obsessive influence derives from those experiences which the child undergoes at a time when we have reason to believe his physical apparatus to be incompletely fitted for accepting them. . . . What a child has experienced and not understood by the time he has reached the age of two he may never again remember, except in his dreams. Only through psychoanalytic treatment will he become aware of those events. At any time in later years, however, they may break into his life with obsessive impulsiveness, direct his actions, force him to like or dislike people, and often decide the choice of his love-object by a preference that so often cannot be rationally defended.   *M & M—Part III, Section II*

Childhood, Phobias in—See *Phobias of Early Childhood.*

Childhood Recollections—The age to which the content of the earliest memories of childhood are usually referred back is the period between the ages of two and four.   *SM*

Various sources force us to assume that the so-called earliest childhood recollections are not true memory traces but later elaborations of the same, elaborations which might have been subjected to the influences of many later psychic forces. Thus, the "childhood reminiscences" of individuals altogether advance to the signification of "concealing memories," and thereby form a noteworthy analogy to the childhood reminiscences as laid down in the legends and myths of nations.

PEL—ch. 4

Childhood, Sexuality in—It seems certain that the newborn child brings with it the germs of sexual feelings which continue to develop for some time and then succumb to a progressive suppression, which may in turn be broken through by the regular advances of the sexual development or may be checked by individual idiosyncrasies. Nothing is known concerning the laws and periodicity of this oscillating course of development. It seems, however, that the sexual life of the child mostly manifests itself in the third or fourth year in some form accessible to observation.   *TCTS II*

The first period of childhood, during which the ego begins to be differentiated from the id, is also the period of early sexual efflorescence which is brought to an end by the period of latency; it can hardly be a matter of chance that this momentous early period subsequently falls a victim to infantile amnesia, and finally that biological modifications in sexual life (such as its diphasic onset to which we have just referred, the disappearance of the periodic character of sexual excitement and the transformation in the relation between female menstruation and male excitation)—that these innovations in sexuality must have been of high importance in the evolution of animals into men.   *OoPA—ch. 7*

See also *Child; Sexuality in Childhood.*

CIRCUMCISION—The primæval custom of circumcision, another symbolic substitute for castration, is only intelligible if it is an expression of subjection to the father's will. (Compare the puberty rites of primitive peoples.)   *OoPa—ch. 7*

CLOTHING—Covering the body, which keeps abreast with civilization, continuously arouses sexual curiosity and serves to supplement the sexual object by uncovering the hidden parts.   *TcTS 1*

[Cf. *Modesty*.]

COMMUNISM—I have no concern with any economic criticisms of the communistic system; but I am able to recognize that psychologically it is founded on an untenable illusion. By abolishing private property one deprives the human love of aggression of one of its instruments, a strong one undoubtedly, but assuredly not the strongest. It in no way alters the individual differences in power and influence which are turned by aggressiveness to its own use, nor does it change the nature of the instinct in any way.   *C & D—ch. 5*

COMPULSION—See *Compulsion Neurosis, Compulsive Acts, Compulsive Ceremonials, Compulsive Symptoms, Repetition-Compulsion.*

COMPULSION TO EAT—There is . . . a compulsion to eat, motivated by a fear of starvation.   *PoA—ch. 1*

COMPULSION NEUROSIS—The symptoms of compulsion neurosis are, broadly speaking, of two kinds and of contradictory purport. Either they are prohibitions or prophylactic measures or atonements, and are thus of a negative character, or they are on the other hand substitute gratifications, very often symbolic in disguise. The situation of origin in the case of compulsion neurosis is in fact none other than that in hysteria, namely, the defense necessary against the libidinal demands of the œdipus complex. Furthermore there seems to be present in every compulsion neurosis a lowermost layer of hysterical symptoms of very early formation. Its subsequent form, however, is then decisively altered by a constitutional factor.   *PoA—ch. 5*

Puberty forms a definite epoch in the development of the compulsion neurosis.   *PoA—ch. 5*

Perhaps in compulsion neurosis, even more clearly than in normal and hysterical cases, we may recognize the castration complex as the motivating force of defense, the strivings of the œdipus complex as that which is defended against.
                                                        PoA—ch. 5

. . . it is precisely the suppressed onanism which in the form of compulsive acts compels an ever furthered approximation to gratification.   *PoA—ch. 5*

See also *Taboo and Compulsion Neurosis.*

COMPULSIVE ACTS—A great many compulsive acts plainly serve as a precaution and an assurance against sexual experience and are therefore phobic in their character.
                                                           PoA—ch. 1

COMPULSIVE CEREMONIALS—Compulsive ceremonials have the intention to "undo" as their second root, their first being to prevent or to forestall some specific thing happening or being repeated. The distinction is easy enough to grasp; precautionary measures are of a rational character, "voiding" or "cancelling" by means of "undoing" of an irrational magical nature.   *PoA—ch. 6*

COMPULSIVE SYMPTOMS—See *Compulsion Neurosis.*

CONCENTRATION—Even in normal persons concentration is utilized to keep at a distance not solely matters of indifference, things that are irrelevant, but in particular things which run inconveniently counter to the matter in hand.
                                                           PoA—ch. 6

CONDENSATION—See *Dream-Condensation.*

CONFESSION AND ANALYSIS—Confession enters into analysis, as its introduction, as it were. But it is far from being the same thing as analysis, and it cannot serve to explain its effect. In confession the sinner tells what he knows, in analysis the neurotic must tell more. Besides, we have no knowledge that the system of confession has developed the power to get rid of direct symptoms of illness.   *QLA—ch. 1*

CONSCIENCE—Conscience is the inner perception of objections to definite wish impulses that exist in us; but the emphasis is put upon the fact that this rejection does not have to depend on anything else, that it is sure of itself. This becomes even plainer in the case of a guilty conscience, where we become aware of the inner condemnation of such acts which realized some of our definite wish impulses.   *T & T—ch. 2*

Conscience is a function we ascribe, among others, to the super-ego; it consists of watching over and judging the actions

and intentions of the ego, exercising the functions of a censor.
C & D—ch. 8

The Super-Ego is the vehicle for the phenomenon we call
"conscience." *QLA—ch. 5*

Conscience and Instinctual Renunciation—Conscience is
the result of instinctual renunciation. *C & D—ch. 7*

CONSCIOUS, CONSCIOUSNESS—Being conscious is an
ephemeral quality which adheres to a psychical process only
temporarily. *M & M—Part III, Section I*

One property of mental life, which may co-exist along with
its other properties or may be absent. *E & I—ch. 1*

For us the state of becoming conscious is a special psychic
act, different from and independent of the process of becoming
fixed or represented, and consciousness appears to us as a sensory organ which perceives a content proceeding from another
source. It may be shown that psychopathology simply cannot
dispense with these fundamental assumptions. *IoD—ch. 4*

It is a complicated matter for a psychical process to become
conscious. *QLA—ch. 2*

Conscious Perception—What rôle is left, in our representation of things, to the phenomenon of consciousness, once
so all-powerful and over-shadowing all else? None other than
that of a sense-organ for the perception of psychic qualities.
According to the fundamental idea of our schematic attempt
we can regard conscious perception only as the function proper
to a special system for which the abbreviated designation *Cs.*
commends itself. *IoD—ch. 7*

Conscious Processes— . . . Most conscious processes
are conscious only for a short period; quite soon they become
latent, though they can easily become conscious again.
NILP—ch. 3

Conscious and Unconscious—There is no need to char-
acterize what we call *conscious:* it is the same as the consciousness of philosophers and of everyday opinion. Everything else
that is mental is in our view *unconscious.* *OoPA—ch. 4*

COUNTER-TRANSFERENCE—The counter-transference,
which arises in the physician as a result of the patient's influence on his unconscious feelings. *FPT*

COUNTER-WISH-DREAM—See *Dream, Counter-Wish.*

CRIMINAL MIND—I must work out an analogy between the criminal and the hysteric. In both we are concerned with a secret, with something hidden. . . . In the case of the criminal it is a secret which he knows and hides from you, but in the case of the hysteric it is a secret hidden from him, a secret he himself does not know.   *PA & CL*

CULTURE—The word "culture" describes the sum of the achievements and institutions which differentiate our lives from those of our animal forebears and serve two purposes, namely, that of protecting humanity against nature and of regulating the relations of human beings among themselves.
                                                                        C & D—ch. 3

The cultural process is the particular modification undergone by the life-process under the influence of the task set before it by Eros and stimulated by Ananke, external necessity.
                                                                        C & D—ch. 8

D

DANGER—An increase in unpleasure which is expected and foreseen is met by a *signal of anxiety;* the occasion of this increase, whether it threatens from without or within, is called a *danger*.   *OoPA—ch. 1*

In relation to the traumatic situation, against which one is helpless, external and internal danger, reality danger and instinctual demand, coincide.   *PoA—ch. 11*

    Danger, Instinctual—See *Danger, Neurotic;* cf.: *Anxiety, True (Real) and Neurotic.*

    Danger, Neurotic—Neurotic danger is one which threatens from an instinctual demand.   *PoA—ch. 11*

    Danger, Real (True)—A real danger is one which threatens from some external object.   *PoA—ch. 11*

In the case of a true danger we develop two reactions: an affective one, the outbreak of anxiety, and action looking to protection from the danger. Presumably the same thing happens in the case of instinctual danger.   *PoA—ch. 11*

DANGER SITUATION—The danger situation is the recognized, remembered and anticipated situation of helplessness.
                                                PoA—ch. 11

What is the kernel, what is the true significance of the danger situation? Evidently it is the estimation of our strength in comparison with its magnitude, the admission of our helplessness in the face of it—of material helplessness in the case of a true danger, of psychic helplessness in that of instinctual danger. Our judgment in this regard will be guided by actual experience; whether one is mistaken in one's evaluation makes no difference to the result. Let us call our experience in a situation of helplessness of this kind a *traumatic* situation; we then have a sufficient basis for distinguishing the *traumatic* from the *danger* situation. Now it is an important advance in self-protection when this traumatic situation of helplessness is not merely awaited but is foreseen, anticipated. Let us call the situation in which resides the cause of this anticipation the danger situation; it is in this latter that the signal of anxiety is given.

PoA—ch. 11

Every danger situation corresponds to a given period of life or stage of development of the psyche, to which it appears appropriate.   *PoA—ch. 9*

Certain of these danger situations survive into a later period of life by means of a modification, in keeping with that later period, of the character of what gives rise to anxiety.

PoA—ch. 9

DEATH

Death, the Child's Concept of—The fear of death is alien to the child. Being dead means, for the child, who has been spared the sight of the suffering that precedes death, much the same as "being gone," and ceasing to annoy the survivors. The child does not distinguish the means by which this absence is brought about, whether by distance, or estrangement, or death.   *IoD—ch. 5*

Death, Fear of—The fear of death is to be regarded as an analogue of the fear of castration, and that the situation to which the ego reacts is the state of being forsaken or deserted by the protecting superego—by the powers of destiny—which puts an end to security against every danger.   *PoA—ch. 7*

DEATH INSTINCT—We may suppose that the final aim of the destructive instinct is to reduce living things to an inorganic state. For this reason we also call it the *death instinct*.

OoPA—ch. 2

DEFENSE—[Cf. *CompulsionNeurosis.*]

DEFENSE (DEFENSIVE) MECHANISM—From the very outset the ego has to try to fulfil its task of acting as an intermediary between the id and the external world in the service of the pleasure principle, to protect the id from the dangers of the external world . . . In this battle on two fronts . . . the ego makes use of various methods of fulfilling its task, i.e. to put it in general terms, of avoiding danger, anxiety and unpleasure. We call these devices *defensive mechanisms*.

AT & I

Defense and Repression—It is convenient to distinguish the general tendency to "defense" from "repression," which is only one of the mechanisms utilized in the service of defense.

PoA—ch. 5

DEFLORATION, PSYCHOLOGICAL EFFECT OF—We may say that the act of defloration has not merely the socially useful result of binding the woman closely to the man; it also liberates an archaic reaction of enmity towards the man, which may assume pathological forms, and often enough expresses itself by inhibitions in the erotic life of the pair, and to which one may ascribe the fact that second marriages so often turn out better than first.

CPL—TV

DEGENERATION—The term, *degeneration,* is open to the objections which may be urged against the promiscuous use of this particular term. It has, in fact, become customary to designate all morbid manifestations not of traumatic or infectious origin as degenerative. It would seem more appropriate not to speak of degeneration: (1) where there are not many marked deviations from the normal; (2) where the capacity for working and living do not in general appear markedly impaired.

TCTS I

DEITIES [Cf. GOD]

Deities, Male—The male gods appear at first as sons by the side of the great mothers; only later do they clearly assume the features of the father. These male gods of polytheism mirror the conditions of patriarchal times.

M & M—Part III, Section I

Deities, Maternal—Probably the mother deities were developed when the matriarchy was being limited, in order to compensate the dethroned mothers.

M & M—Part III, Section I

The infantile assumption of the maternal penis is . . . the common source of origin for the androgynous formation of the maternal deities like the Egyptian goddess Mut.

LDV—ch. 3

DÉJÀ RACONTÉ—The *Déjà raconté* feeling, the illusion that something has already been related during the psychoanalytic treatment, which is especially interesting. The patient asserts with all subjective signs of certainty, that he previously related this definite episode. The physician, however, is sure of the contrary and, as a rule, can convince the patient of it. The explanation of this interesting phenomenon is undoubtedly based on the fact that the patient had the impulse and intention of imparting this memory, but failed to execute it, and that he now puts the memory of the first resolution as a substitute for the second feeling.   *PEL—ch. 10*

DÉJA VU—I believe that it is wrong to designate the feeling of having experienced something before as an illusion. On the contrary, in such moments, something is really touched that we have already experienced, only we cannot consciously recall the latter because it never was conscious. In the latter, the feeling of *Déjà vu* corresponds to the memory of an unconscious phantasy. There are unconscious phantasies (or day-dreams) just as there are similar conscious creations, which everyone knows from personal experience.   *PEL—ch. 10*

DENIAL—If we wish to differentiate between what happens to the *idea* as distinct from the *affect,* we can restrict "repression" to relate to the affect; the correct word for what happens to the idea is then "denial."   *Fet*

DEPRESSION, CYCLICAL—There are people the general colour of whose mood oscillates periodically from an excessive depression through some kind of intermediate state to an exalted sense of well-being. It has become the custom to consider these cases as not being psychogenic.   *GPAE—ch. 11*

DISPLACEMENT OF MEMORY, REGRESSIVE—See *Memory, Concealment of.*

DELUSION—It has long been recognized that delusions contain a piece of forgotten truth, which had at its return to put up with being distorted and misunderstood, and that the compulsive conviction appertaining to the delusion emanates from this core of truth and spreads to the errors that enshroud it.   *M & M—Part III, Section I*

    Delusion of Observation—One group of them [psychotics] suffer what we call delusions of observation. They complain to us that they suffer continually, and in their most intimate actions, from the observation of unknown powers or persons, and they have hallucinations in which they hear these persons announcing the results of their observations: "now he is going to say this, now he is dressing himself to go out," and so on. Such observation is not the same as persecution, but it is not far removed from it.   *NILP—ch. 3*

Delusion, Psychiatric—The psychiatric delusion also contains a particle of truth; the patient's conviction issues from this and extends to the whole delusional fabrication surrounding it. *M & M—Part III, Section II*

DREAD—Anxiety . . . is endowed with a certain character of indefiniteness and objectlessness; correct usage even changes its name when it has found an object, and in that case speaks instead of *dread*. *PoA—ch. 11*

Dread in an individual is provoked either by the greatness of a danger or by the cessation of emotional ties (libidinal cathexes); the latter is the case of neurotic dread. *GPAE—ch. 5*

DREAM—A dream is, among other things, a *projection:* an externalization of an internal process. *MSTD*

Dreams are absolutely egotistic. *IoD—ch. 6*

All our dreams are preponderantly visual. *PEL—ch. 4*

Dreams, from above and from below—Dreams from below are those which are provoked by the strength of an unconscious (repressed) wish which has found a means of being represented in some of the day's residues. Dreams from above correspond to thoughts or intentions of the day before which have contrived during the night to obtain reinforcement from repressed material which is debarred from the ego. *TPDI*

Dreams, Anxiety—Anxiety dreams do not contradict the wish-fulfilling function of the dream. *NILP—ch. 1*

Anxiety in dreams is an anxiety-problem and not a dream-problem. *IoD—ch. 7*

The anxiety in dreams may of course be of a psychoneurotic character, originating in psycho-sexual excitation, in which case, the anxiety corresponds to repressed libido. Then this anxiety, like the whole anxiety-dream, has the significance of a neurotic symptom, and we stand at the dividing-line where the wish-fulfilling tendency of dreams is frustrated. But in other anxiety-dreams the feeling of anxiety comes from somatic sources (as in the case of persons suffering from pulmonary or cardiac trouble, with occasional difficulty in breathing), and then it is used to help such strongly suppressed wishes to attain fulfilment in a dream, the dreaming of which from psychic motives would have resulted in the same release of anxiety. It is not difficult to reconcile these two apparently contradictory cases. When two psychic formations, an affective inclination and a conceptual content, are intimately connected, either one being actually present will evoke the other, even in a dream; now the anxiety of somatic origin evokes the suppressed conceptual content, now it is the released conceptual content, accompanied by sexual excitement, which causes the release of anxiety. In the one case it may be said that a somatically determined affect is psychically interpreted; in the other case all is of psychic origin, but the content which has been suppressed is easily replaced by a somatic interpretation which fits the anxiety.   *IoD—ch. 5*

Dreams, Anxiety of Examination—We have had increasing confirmation of the fact that the anxiety-dream of examination occurs when the dreamer is anticipating a responsible task on the following day, with the possibility of disgrace.
     IoD—ch. 5

Dreams, Archaic Heritage in—See *Dream-Formation, Share of the Id in*.

Dreams, Counter-Wish—In the sexual constitution of many persons there is a masochistic component, which has arisen through the conversion of the aggressive, sadistic component into its opposite. Such people are called "ideal" masochists if they seek pleasure not in the bodily pain which may be inflicted upon them, but in humiliation and psychic chastisement. It is obvious that such persons may have counter-wish-dreams and disagreeable dreams, yet these are for them nothing more than wish-fulfillments, which satisfy their masochistic inclinations.   *IoD—ch. 4*

Dreams, Composite Formation in—The possibility of creating composite formations is one of the chief causes of the fantastic character so common in dreams, in that it introduces into the dream-content elements which could never have been objects of perception. The psychic process which occurs in the creation of composite formations is obviously the same as that which we employ in conceiving or figuring a dragon or a centaur in our waking senses. The only difference is that in the fantastic creations of waking life the impression intended is itself the decisive factor, while the composite formation in the dream is determined by a factor—the common feature in the dream-thoughts—which is independent of its form. Composite formations in dreams may be achieved in a great many different ways. *IoD—ch. 6*

Dreams, Childhood Experiences in—If we turn from the manifest dream-content to the dream-thoughts which are revealed only on analysis, the experiences of childhood may be found to recur even in dreams whose content would not have led us to suspect anything of the sort. . . . *The child with all his impulses survives in the dream.* As a rule, of course, a scene from childhood is represented in the manifest dream-content only by an allusion, and must be disentangled from the dream by interpretation. The citation of examples of this kind cannot be very convincing, because any guarantee that they are really experiences of childhood is lacking; if they belong to an earlier period of life, they are no longer recognized by our memory. The conclusion that such childish experiences recur at all in dreams is justified in psychoanalytic work by a great number of factors, which in their combined results appear to be sufficiently reliable. But when, for the purposes of dream-interpretation such references to childish experiences are torn out of their context they may not perhaps seem very impressive. *IoD—ch. 5*

Dreams, Children's—The dreams of little children are often simple fulfilments of wishes, and for this reason are, as compared with the dreams of adults, by no means interesting. They present no problem to be solved, but they are invaluable as affording proof that the dream, in its inmost essence, is the fulfilment of a wish. I have been able to collect several examples of such dreams from the material furnished by my own children. *IoD—ch. 3*

Dreams, Classification of—We have kept our theory intact by dividing dreams into wish-dreams, anxiety-dreams, and punishment-dreams. *NILP—ch. 1*

Dreams, Composite Formation in—*Similarity, agreement, community,* are quite generally expressed in dreams by contraction into a *unity,* which is either already found in the dream-material or is newly created. The first case may be referred to as *identification,* the second as *composition.* Identification is used where the dream is concerned with persons, composition where things constitute the material to be unified; but compositions are also made of persons. Localities are often treated as persons. *IoD—ch. 6*

Dreams as Compromise Structures—It must not be for-gotten that dreams are invariably the product of a conflict, that they are a kind of compromise structure. Something that is a satisfaction for the unconscious id may for that very reason be a cause of anxiety for the ego.   *OoPA*

Dreams, Context of—All the dreams of one night belong to the same context; but it is by no means immaterial whether these dreams appear to the dreamer as a continuum, or whether they are organized in several pieces, and if so in how many. The number of pieces often corresponds to the same number of distinct nodal points in the chain of thoughts, which make up the latent dream-thoughts; or it may correspond to forces in the mental life of the dreamer which are struggling with one another, and each of which finds its main (though not its exclusive) expression in one particular part of the dream. A short introductory dream and a long main dream often stand to each other in the relation of condition and consequent; of this you will find a very clear example in the old lectures. A dream which the dreamer describes as "some-how interpolated" really corresponds to a dependent clause in the dream-thoughts.   *NILP—ch. 1*

Dreams, Critical Faculty in—Everything in dreams which occurs as the apparent functioning of the critical faculty is to be regarded, not as the intellectual performance of the dream-work, but as belonging to the substance of the dream-thoughts, and it has found its way from these, as a completed structure, into the manifest dream-content.   *IoD—ch. 6*

Dreams, Displacement in—See *Dream-Displacement*.

Dreams, Distortion in—See *Dream-Distortion*.

Dreams, Exhibition—The nucleus of an exhibition-dream is furnished by one's own person which is seen not as that of a child, but as it exists in the present, and by the idea of scanty clothing which emerges indistinctly, owing to the super-imposition of so many later situations of being partially clothed, or out of consideration for the censorship; to these elements are added the persons in whose presence one is ashamed. Strangely enough, those persons who are the objects of our sexual interest in childhood are omitted from all reproductions in dreams, in hysteria or in obsessional neurosis; paranoia alone restores the spectators, and is fanatically convinced of their presence, although they remain unseen. Furthermore, repression finds a place in the exhibition-dream. For the disagreeable sensation of the dream is, of course, the reaction on the part of the second physchic instance to the fact that the exhibitionistic scene—which has been condemned by the censorship has nevertheless succeeded in presenting itself. The only way to avoid this sensation would be to refrain from reviving the scene. *IoD—ch. 5*

Dreams, Effect of External Stimuli on—The stimuli which occur during sleep are elaborated into a wish-fulfilment, of which the other components are the psychic remnants of daily experience with which we are already familiar. This combination, however, is not inevitable; we have seen that more than one kind of behaviour toward the physical stimuli received during sleep is possible. Where this combination is effected, a conceptual material for the dream-content has been found which will represent both kinds of dream-sources, the somatic as well as the psychic.

The nature of the dream is not altered when somatic material is added to the psychic dream-sources; it still remains a wish-fulfilment, no matter how its expression is determined by the actual material available.

I should like to find room here for a number of peculiarities which are able to modify the significance of external stimuli for the dream. I imagine that co-operation of individual, physiological and accidental factors, which depend on the circumstances of the moment, determines how one will behave in individual cases of more intensive objective stimulation during sleep; habitual or accidental profundity of sleep, in conjunction with the intensity of the stimulus, will in one case make it possible so to suppress the stimulus that it will not disturb the sleeper, while in another case it will force the sleeper to wake, or will assist the attempt to subdue the stimulus by weaving it into the texture of the dream. In accordance with the multiplicity of these constellations, external objective stimuli will be expressed more rarely or more frequently in the case of one person than in that of another. *IoD—ch. 5*

Dreams of Falling—Dreams of *falling* are more frequently characterized by anxiety. Their interpretation, when they occur in women, offers no difficulty, because they nearly always accept the symbolic meaning of falling, which is a circumlocution for giving way to an erotic temptation. We have not yet exhausted the infantile sources of the dream of falling; nearly all children have fallen occasionally, and then been picked up and fondled; if they fell out of bed at night, they were picked up by the nurse and taken into her bed.

IoD—ch. 6

I have good reasons for rejecting the explanation that it is the state of our dermal sensations during sleep, the sensation of the movements of the lungs, etc., that evokes dreams of flying and falling. I see that these very sensations have been reproduced from the memory to which the dream refers—and that they are, therefore, dream-content and not dream-sources.

IoD—ch. 5

Dreams of Fire—The interpretation of dreams of *fire* justifies a prohibition of the nursery, which forbids children to "play with fire" so that they may not wet the bed at night. These dreams also are based on reminiscences of the *enuresis nocturna* of childhood. In my *Fragment of an Analysis of Hysteria* I have given the complete analysis and synthesis of such a dream of fire in connection with the infantile history of the dreamer, and have shown for the representation of what maturer impulses this infantile material has been utilized.

IoD—ch. 6

Dreams of Flying—Why do so many people dream of flying? Psychoanalysis answers this question by stating that to fly or to be a bird in the dream is nothing but a concealment of another wish to the recognition of which we are led by more than one linguistic or real bridge. When the inquisitive child is told that a big bird like the stork brings the little children, when the ancients have formed the phallus winged . . . all these facts are only small fragments from a large collection which teaches us that the wish to be able to fly signifies in the dream nothing but the longing for the ability of sexual accomplishment. This is an early infantile wish. When the grown-up recalls his childhood, it appears to him as a joyful time, in which one is happy for the moment and looks to the future without any wishes; it is for this reason that he envies children. But the children themselves, if they could inform us about it, would probably give us different reports. It seems that childhood is not that blissful idyl into which we later distort it, that on the contrary children are lashed through the years of childhood by the wish to become big, and to imitate the grown-ups. This wish instigates all their playing. If in the course of their sexual investigation children feel that the grown-up knows something wonderful concerning the mysterious and yet so important realm that they are prohibited from knowing or doing, they are seized with a violent wish to know it, and dream of it in the form of flying, or prepare this disguise of the wish for their later flying dreams. Thus aviation, which has attained its aim in our times, has also its infantile erotic roots.

LDV—ch. 6

Dreams, Forgetting of—See *Forgetting of Dreams.*

Dreams, Function of—Under certain conditions the dream can only achieve its end in a very incomplete way, or has to abandon it entirely; an unconscious fixation to the trauma seems to head the list of these obstacles to the dream-function. The sleeper has to dream, because the nightly relaxation of repression allows the upward thrust of the traumatic fixation to become active; but sometimes his dream-work, which endeavours to change the memory traces of the traumatic event into a wish-fulfilment, fails to operate. In these circumstances the result is that one becomes sleepless; one gives up all idea of sleep because of one's fear of the failure of the dream-function. The traumatic neurosis is an extreme case, but one must also attribute a traumatic character to infantile experiences as well; so one need not be surprised if lesser disturbances of the function of the dream occur in other circumstances.

NILP—ch. 1

Dreams, Inversion in—The dream-work is able to dispose of the affects of the dream-thoughts in yet another way than by admitting them or reducing them to zero. *It can transform them into their opposites.*

IoD—ch. 6

Inversion, or transformation into the opposite, is one of the most favoured and most versatile methods of representation which the dream-work has at its disposal.

Besides the inversion of content, the temporal inversion must not be overlooked.

IoD—ch. 6

Dreams take the liberty of representing any element whatever by its desired opposite, so that it is at first impossible to tell, in respect of any element which is capable of having an opposite, whether it is contained in the dream-thoughts in the negative or the positive sense.

IoD—ch. 6

Dream, Manifest—We call what one usually refers to as the dream, the dream-text or the *manifest* dream.

NILP—ch. 1

Dreams, Material of—The dream may select its material from any period of life, provided only that a chain of thought leads back from the experiences of the day of the dream (the "recent" impressions) of that earlier period.   *IoD—ch. 5*

Dream as a Pathological Product—The dream is a pathological product, the first member of the series which includes the hysterical symptom, the obsession and the delusion among its members; it is differentiated from the others by its transitoriness and by the fact that it occurs under conditions which are part of normal life.   *NILP—ch. 1*

Dreams, Prophetic—The belief in prophetic dreams numbers many adherents, because it can be supported by the fact that some things really so happen in the future as they were previously foretold by the wish of the dream. But in this, there is little to be wondered at, as many far-reaching deviations may be regularly demonstrated between a dream and the fulfillment which the credulity of the dreamer prefers to neglect.   *PEL—ch. 10*

There can, indeed, be no doubt that there are such things as prophetic dreams, in the sense that their content gives some sort of picture of the future; the only question is whether these predictions coincide to any noticeable extent with what really happens subsequently.   *OSD*

Dream as a Psychosis—A dream, then, is a psychosis, with all the absurdities, delusions and illusions of a psychosis. No doubt it is a psychosis which has only a short duration, which is harmless and even performs a useful function, which is brought about with the subject's consent and is ended by an act of his will. Nevertheless it *is* a psychosis, and we learn from it that even so deep-going a modification of mental life as this can be undone and can give place to normal functioning.   *OoPA—ch. 6*

Dreams, Punishment—Even punishment-dreams are wish-fulfilments, but they do not fulfil the wishes of the instinctual impulses, but those of the critical, censuring and punishing function of the mind. If we are faced with a pure punishment-dream, a simple mental operation will enable us to reinstate the wish-dream to which the punishment-dream was the proper rejoinder; on account of this repudiation, the punishment-dream has appeared in place of the wish-dream as the manifest one.   *NILP—ch. 1*

Dreams, Secondary Elaboration in—There is to be considered a more or less non-constant factor, the so-called secondary elaboration, that makes its appearance after the dream has come into consciousness as an object of perception. When the dream has come into consciousness, we treat it in exactly the same way that we treat any content of perception; we try to fill in the gaps, we add connecting links, and often enough we let ourselves in for serious misunderstandings.

NILP—ch. 1

Dream and Its Relationship to Sleep—Throughout the whole of our sleep we are just as certain that we are dreaming as we are certain that we are sleeping. *IoD—ch. 7*

Every dream is an *attempt* to put aside a disturbance of sleep by means of a wish-fulfillment. The dream is thus the guardian of sleep. This attempt can be more or less completely successful; it can also fail—in which case the sleeper wakes up, apparently aroused by the dream itself. *OoPA—ch. 5*

Dreams, Influence of Somatic Stimuli on—The general aggregate of bodily sensation must undoubtedly be included among the dominant dream-stimuli of internal bodily origin. Not that it is capable of supplying the dream-content; but it forces the dream-thoughts to make a choice from the material destined to serve the purpose of representation in the dream-content, inasmuch as it brings within easy reach that part of the material which is adapted to its own character, and holds the rest at a distance. Moreover, this general feeling, which survives from the preceding day, is of course connected with the psychic residues that are significant for the dream. Moreover, this feeling itself may be either maintained or overcome in the dream, so that it may, if it is painful, veer round into its opposite. *IoD—ch. 5*

If the external nerve-stimuli and the inner bodily stimuli are sufficiently intense to compel psychic attention, they represent —that is, if they result in dreaming at all, and not in waking—a fixed point for dream-formation, a nucleus in the dream-material, for which an appropriate wish-fulfilment is sought, just as well as mediating ideas between two psychical dream-stimuli are sought. To this extent it is true of a number of dreams that the somatic element dictates the dream-content. In this extreme case even a wish that is not actually present may be aroused for the purpose of dream-formation. But the dream cannot do otherwise than represent a wish in some situation as fulfilled; it is, as it were, confronted with the task of discovering what wish can be represented as fulfilled by the given sensation. Even if this given material is of a painful or disagreeable character, yet it is not unserviceable for the purposes of dream-formation. The psychic life has at its disposal even wishes whose fulfilment evokes displeasure, which seems a contradiction, but becomes perfectly intelligible if we take into account the presence of two sorts of psychic instance and the censorship that subsists between them. If sensations of a disagreeable character which originate from somatic sources are present during sleep, this constellation is utilized by the dream-activity to procure the fulfilment—with more or less maintenance of the censorship—of an otherwise suppressed wish. *IoD—ch. 5*

Dreams, Sources of—The source of a dream may be:—
(*a*) A recent and psychologically significant event which is directly represented in the dream.
(*b*) Several recent and significant events, which are combined by the dream into a single whole.
(*c*) One or more recent and significant events, which are represented in the dream-content by allusion to a contemporary but indifferent event.
(*d*) A subjectively significant experience (recollection, train of thought), which is *constantly* represented in the dream by allusion to a recent but indifferent impression. *IoD—ch. 5*

Dreams, Speech in—When a spoken utterance, expressly distinguished as such from a thought, occurs in a dream, it is an invariable rule that the dream-speech has originated from a remembered speech in the dream-material. The wording of the speech has either been preserved in its entirety or has been slightly altered in expression; frequently the dream-speech is pieced together from different recollections of spoken remarks; the wording has remained the same, but the sense has perhaps become ambiguous, or differs from the wording. Not infrequently the dream-speech serves merely as an allusion to an incident in connection with which the remembered speech was made. *IoD—ch. 6*

Dreams of Swimming—People who dream often, and with great enjoyment, of *swimming,* cleaving the waves, etc., have usually been bed-wetters, and they now repeat in the dream a pleasure which they have long since learned to forego. *IoD—ch. 6*

Dreams, Theory of—This theory occupies a peculiar position in the history of psycho-analysis; it marks a turning-point. With the theory of dreams, analysis passed from being a psycho-therapeutic method to being a psychology of the depths of human nature.   *NILP—ch. 1*

Dreams, Unification Compulsion in—If the day has brought us two or more experiences which are worthy to evoke a dream, the dream will blend the allusion of both into a single whole: it obeys *a compulsion to make them into a single whole*. I am persuaded to advance the proposition that a dream works under a kind of compulsion which forces it to combine into a unified whole all the sources of dream-stimulation which are offered to it.   *IoD—ch. 5*

Dream and Wish-Fulfillment—I believe that the *conscious wish becomes effective in exciting a dream only when it succeeds in arousing a similar unconscious wish which reinforces it.*   *IoD—ch. 7*

The dream is the (disguised) fulfilment of a (suppressed, repressed) wish.   *IoD—ch. 4*

In every dream an instinctual wish is displayed as fulfilled.   *NILP—ch. 1*

Children's dreams leave us in no doubt that a wish unfulfilled during the day may instigate a dream.   *IoD—ch. 7*

Perhaps this collection will suffice to prove that frequently, and under the most complex conditions, dreams may be noted which can be understood only as wish-fulfilments, and which present their content without concealment. In most cases these are short and simple dreams, and they stand in pleasant contrast to the confused and overloaded dream-compositions which have almost exclusively attracted the attention of the writers on the subject. But it will repay us if we give some time to the examination of these simple dreams. The simplest dreams of all are, I suppose, to be expected in the case of children whose psychic activities are certainly less complicated than those of adults.   *IoD—ch. 3*

DREAM-CENSOR—The conflict of two psychic factors, which we—roughly—call the repressed unconscious and the conscious, dominates our lives, and the resistance against the interpretation of dreams, the hall-mark of the dream-censorship, is none other than the repression-resistance which keeps these two factors apart.   *NILP—ch. 1*

The fact of dream-censorship shows that enough repressive resistance remains operative even during sleep.   *NILP—ch. 1*

The resistance which we come across during the process of dream-interpretation must play some part in the formation of the dream as well. . . . Resistance is the sure sign of a conflict. There must be a force present which is trying to express something, and another which is striving to prevent its expression. What comes into being as the manifest dream may, therefore, be regarded as comprising all the solutions to which the battle between these two opposing forces can be reduced. At one point one of the forces may have been able to get through what it wanted to say, at another the counteracting force may have succeeded in abolishing the intended communication entirely, or may have substituted for it something which betrays no sign of it. The most usual cases, and those which are the most characteristic of the process of dream-formation, are those in which the conflict results in a compromise, so that the communicating force can indeed say what it wants to say, but not in the way it wants to say it; it is toned down, distorted and made unrecognizable. If therefore the dream does not faithfully represent the dream-thoughts, if a process of interpretation is necessary to bridge the gulf between the two, this is the result of the counteracting, inhibiting and restraining force whose existence we have inferred from perceiving the resistance in dream-interpretation. So long as we regarded the dream as an isolated phenomenon, independent of other psychological formations which are allied to it, we called this force the *dream-censor*.

NILP—ch. 1

DREAM-CONDENSATION—The laws governing unconscious processes, which come to light in this manner, are remarkable enough and suffice to explain the greater part of what seems strange to us about dreams. Above all there is a striking tendency to *condensation,* an inclination to form fresh unities out of elements which in our waking thoughts we should certainly have kept separate. As a consequence of this, a single element of the manifest dream often stands for a whole number of latent dream-thoughts, as though it were a combined allusion to all of them; and in general the dimensions of a manifest dream are extraordinarily small in comparison with the wealth of material from which it has sprung.   *OoPA—ch. 5*

On other occasions and even much more frequently, the condensation work of the dream produces no compositions, but

pictures which closely resemble an object or person up to a
certain addition or variation which comes from another source.
WRU—ch. II

DREAM-CONTENT—The peculiar mode of operation,
whose most striking function we recognize in the dream content, should not be attributed only to the sleeping state of the
psychic life, when we possess abundant proof of its activity
during the waking state in faulty actions. The same connection
also forbids us from assuming that these psychic processes
which impress us as abnormal and strange, are determined by
deep-seated decay of psychic activity or by morbid state of
function. *PEL—ch. 10*

For us a new psychic material interposes itself between the
dream-content and the results of our investigations: the *latent*
dream-content, or dream-thoughts, which are obtained only by
our method. We develop the solution of the dream from this
latent content, and not from the manifest dream-content. The
dream-content appears to us as a translation of the dream-
thoughts into another mode of expression, whose symbols and
laws of composition we must learn by comparing the origin
with the translation. *IoD—ch. 6*

DREAM-DAY—In every dream we may find some reference
to the experience of the preceding day. [See also: *Dream-Interpretation, Technique of.*] *IoD—ch. 5*

DREAM-DISPLACEMENT—It becomes very probable that
a psychic force expresses itself in the dream-work which, on the
one hand, strips the elements of the high psychic value of their
intensity and, on the other hand, *by means of overdetermina-
tion,* creates new significant values from elements of slight
value, which new values then make their way into the dream-
content. Now if this is the method of procedure, there has
occurred in the process of dream-formation a *transference and
displacement of the psychic intensities* of the individual elements, from which results the textual difference between the
dream-content and the thought-content. The process which we
here assume to be operative is actually the most essential part
of the dream-work; it may fitly be called *dream-displacement.
Dream-displacement and dream-condensation* are the two
craftsmen to whom we may chiefly ascribe the structure of
the dream.

I think it will be easy to recognize the psychic force which expresses itself in dream-displacement. The result of this displacement is that the dream-content no longer has any likeness to the nucleus of the dream-thoughts, and the dream reproduces only a distorted form of the dream-wish in the unconscious. But we are already acquainted with dream-distortion; we have traced it back to the censorship which one psychic instance in the psychic life exercises over another. Dream-displacement is one of the chief means of achieving this distortion. *Is fecit, cui profuit.* We must assume that dream-displacement is brought about by the influence of this censorship, the endopsychic defence.   *IoD—ch. 6*

Displacement usually occurs in such a way that a coulourless and abstract expression of the dream-thought is exchanged for one that is pictorial and concrete.   *IoD—ch. 6*

DREAM-DISTORTION—The dream-content takes up remnants of trivial experiences as a manifestation of *dream-distortion* (by displacement), and we have recognized this dream-distortion as the work of a censorship operating between the two psychic instances.   *IoD—ch. 5*

The study of dream-work affords us an excellent example of the way in which unconscious material from the id—originally unconscious and repressed unconscious alike—forces itself upon the ego, becomes preconscious and, owing to the efforts of the ego, undergoes the modifications which we call *dream-distortion.* There are no features of the dream which cannot be explained in this fashion.   *OoPA—ch. 5*

I regard the attribution of dream-distortion to the censorship as the central point of my conception of the dream.   *IoD—ch. 6*

There are, of course, dreams which are undisguised wish-fulfilments. Wherever a wish-fulfilment is unrecognizable and disguised there must be present a tendency to defend oneself against this wish, and in consequence of this defence the wish is unable to express itself save in distorted form.

The detailed correspondence between the phenomena of censorship and the phenomena of dream-distortion justifies us in presupposing similar conditions for both. We should then assume that in every human being there exist, as the primary cause of dream-formation, two psychic forces (tendencies or systems), one of which forms the wish expressed by the dream, while the other exercises a censorship over this dream-wish, thereby enforcing on it a distortion.   *IoD—ch. 4*

Dream-Distortion as Prevention of Anxiety—An anxiety-dream occurs only when the censorship is entirely or partially overpowered, and on the other hand, the overpowering of the censorship is facilitated when the actual sensation of anxiety is already present from somatic sources. It thus becomes obvious for what purpose the censorship performs its office and practises dream-distortion; it does so *in order to prevent the development of anxiety or other forms of painful affect.*   *IoD—ch. 5*

DREAM-FORMATION—The unconscious impulse is the real creator of the dream, it provides the psychic energy required for its formation.   *NILP—ch. 1*

Roughly speaking, one can distinguish three general stages in the formation of the dream: first, the transference of the conscious day remnants into the unconscious, a transference in which the conditions of the sleeping state must co-operate; secondly, the actual dream-work in the unconscious; and thirdly, the regression of the elaborated dream material to the region of perception, whereby the dream becomes conscious.

The forces participating in the dream-formation may be recognized as the following: the wish to sleep; the sum of cathexis which still clings to the day remnants after the depression brought about by the state of sleep; the pscyhic energy of the unconscious wish forming the dream; and the opposing force of the *"censorship,"* which exercises its authority in our waking state, and is not entirely abolished during sleep. The task of dream-formation is, above all, to overcome the inhibition of the censorship, and it is just this task that is fulfilled by the displacement of the psychic energy within the material of the dream-thoughts.   *WRU—ch. VI*

Let me repeat the stages of dream-formation. The introduction: the wish to sleep, the voluntary withdrawal from the outside world. Two things follow from this: firstly, the possibility for older and more primitive modes of activity to manifest themselves, *i.e.* regression; and secondly, the decrease of the repression-resistance which weighs on the unconscious. As a result of this latter feature an opportunity for dream-formation presents itself, which is seized upon by the factors which are the occasion of the dream; that is to say, the internal and external stimuli which are in activity. The dream which thus eventuates is already a compromise-formation; it has a double function: it is on the one hand in conformity with the ego ('ego-syntonic'), since it subserves the wish to sleep by draining off the stimuli which would otherwise disturb it, while on the other hand it allows to a repressed impulse the satisfaction which is possible in these circumstances in the form of an hallucinatory wish-fulfilment. The whole process of dream-formation, which is permitted by the sleeping ego, is however, under the control of the censorship, a control which is exercised by what is left of the forces of repression. I cannot explain the process more simply; it is not in itself simpler than that.   *NILP—ch. 1*

See also *Dream-Censor, Dream-Work*.

Dream-Formation, Share of the Id in—The evidence of the share taken by the unconscious id in the formation of dreams is abundant and convincing. (*a*) Memory is far more comprehensive in dreams than in waking life. Dreams bring up recollections which the dreamer has forgotten, which are inaccessible to him when he is awake. (*b*) Dreams make an unlimited use of linguistic symbols, the meaning of which is for the most part unknown to the dreamer. Our experience, however, enables us to establish their sense. They probably originate from earlier phases in the development of speech. (*c*) Memory very often reproduces in dreams impressions from the dreamer's early childhood of which we can definitely assert not only that they had been forgotten but that they had become unconscious owing to repression. This is the explanation of the help—usually indispensable—afforded to us by dreams when, in the course of the analytic treatment of the neuroses, we attempt to reconstruct the early life of the dreamer. (*d*) Beyond this, dreams bring to light material which could not originate either from the dreamer's adult life or from his forgotten childhood. We are obliged to regard it as part of the *archaic heritage* which a child brings with him into the world, before any experience of his own, as a result of the experiences of his ancestors.   *OoPA—ch. 5*

Dream-Formation, the Role of Sleep in—The state of sleep makes dream-formation possible by reducing the endopsychic censorship.   *IoD—ch. 7*

DREAM-INTERPRETATION—There is a psychological technique which makes it possible to interpret dreams, and on the application of this technique, every dream will reveal itself as a psychological structure, full of significance, and one which may be assigned to a specific place in the psychic activities of the waking state.   *IoD—ch. 1*

The dream often appears to have several meanings; not only may several wish-fulfilments be combined in it, as our examples show, but one meaning or one wish-fulfilment may conceal another, until in the lowest stratum one comes upon the fulfilment of a wish from the earliest period of childhood; and here again it may be questioned whether the word "often" at the beginning of this sentence may not more correctly be replaced by "constantly."   *IoD—ch. 5*

We have got to turn the manifest dream into the latent dream, and we have to show how the latter became the former in the mental life of the dreamer. The first bit is a practical problem, it comes under the heading of *dream-interpretation,* and requires a technique; the second is a theoretical problem, its solution should be the explanation of the hypothetical *dream-work,* and can only be a theory.   *NILP—ch. 1*

It is impossible to interpret a dream unless one knows the relevant associations of the dreamer.   *NILP—ch. 1*

Dream-Interpretation, Resistance in—The work of interpretation is carried on in the face of resistance, which may vary from an imperceptible amount to an amount so great that we cannot overcome it—at any rate with the means which are at present at our disposal. We are right in supposing that the longer and the more circuitous the chain of associations, the stronger is the resistance. And in the forgetting of dreams, too, we sense the same influence.   *NILP—ch. 1*

Dreams, Semantics in—We cannot dismiss the conjecture, which forces itself on us psychiatrists, that we should understand the language of dreams better and translate it more easily if we knew more about the development of language.
ASPW

Dream-Interpretation, Technique of—We ask the dreamer as well to free himself from the impression of the manifest dream, to switch his attention from the dream as a whole to individual parts of its content, and to tell us one after another the things that occur to him in connection with these parts, what associations come into his mind when he turns his mental eye on to each of them separately. In what order shall we get the patient to take the parts of his dream? Here we have a variety of courses open to us. We can simply follow the chronological order in which the dream has been presented to us in description. That is what one might call the strictest, the classical method. Or we can ask the dreamer to look for the *residue of the previous day* in his dream, because experience has taught us that in almost every dream is incorporated a memory trace of, or an allusion to, an event (or it may be several events) of the previous day [the "dream day"]; and if we follow up these links we often discover all of a sudden the bridge from the apparently remote dream-world to the real life of the patient. Or else we tell him to begin with those elements in the dream-content which have struck him on account of their clarity and sensuous force. We happen to know that it is particularly easy for him to obtain associations to such elements. It makes no difference by which of these ways we choose to reach the associations we are looking for. But let us have no misunderstanding. The associations to the dream are not the latent dream-thoughts. These are contained, but not completely contained, in the associations.   *NILP—ch. 1*

DREAM-TEXT—See *Dream, Manifest.*

DREAM-THOUGHTS—The *content* of the dream-thoughts is reproduced by the apparent thinking in our dreams, but not *the relations of the dream-thoughts to one another,* in the determination of which relations thinking consists.   *IoD—ch. 6*

Dream-Thoughts, Latent—We call what we are looking for, what we, as it were, suspect to lie behind the dream, the *latent* dream-thoughts.   *NILP—ch. 1*

Their dominating element is the repressed impulse, which has obtained some kind of expression, toned down and disguised though it may be, by associating itself with stimuli which happen to be there by tucking itself in the residue of the day before.   *NILP—ch. 1*

[Cf. also *Dream-Interpretation, Technique of.*]

DREAM-WORK—We have our distinction between *manifest* dream-material and *latent* dream-thoughts. The process which produces the former out of the latter is described as *dream-work.*   *OoPA—ch. 5*

The function of the dream-work may be described in the following manner: A structure of thoughts, mostly very complicated, which has been built up during the day and not brought to settlement—a day remnant—clings firmly even during night to the energy which it had assumed—the underlying center of interest—and thus threatens to disturb sleep. This day remnant is transformed into a dream by the dream-work and in this way rendered harmless to sleep. But in order to make possible its employment by the dream-work, this day remnant must be capable of being cast into the form of a wish, a condition that is not difficult to fulfill. The wish emanating from the dream-thoughts forms the first step and later on the nucleus of the dream. Experience gained from analyses—not the theory of the dream—teaches us that with children a fond wish left from the waking state suffices to evoke a dream, which is coherent and senseful, but almost always short, and easily recognizable as a "wish fulfillment."   *WRU—ch. VI*

The psychic activity in dream-formation resolves itself into two achievements: the production of the dream-thoughts and the transformation of these into the dream-content. The dream-thoughts are perfectly accurate, and are formed with all the psychic profusion of which we are capable; they belong to the thoughts which have not become conscious, from which our conscious thoughts also result by means of a certain transposition. There is doubtless much in them that is worth knowing, and also mysterious, but these problems have no particular relation to our dreams, and cannot claim to be treated under the head of dream-problems. On the other hand we have the process which changes the unconscious thoughts into the dream-content, which is peculiar to the dream-life and characteristic of it. Now, this peculiar dream-work is much farther removed from the pattern of waking thought than has been supposed by even the most decided depreciators of the psychic activity in dream-formation. It is not so much that it is more negligent, more incorrect, more forgetful, more incomplete than waking thought; it is something altogether different, qualitatively, from waking thought, and cannot therefore be compared with it. It does not think, calculate, or judge at all, but limits itself to the work of transformation. It may be exhaustively described if we do not lose sight of the conditions which its product must satisfy. This product, the dream, has above all to be withdrawn from the censorship, and to this end the dream-work makes use of the *displacement of psychic intensities,* even to the transvaluation of all psychic values; thoughts must be exclusively or predominantly reproduced in the material of visual and acoustic memory-traces, and from this requirement there proceeds the *regard of the dream-work for representability,* which it satisfies by fresh displacements. Greater intensities have (probably) to be produced than are at the disposal of the night dream-thoughts, and this purpose is served by the extensive *condensation* to which the constituents of the dream-thoughts are subjected. Little attention is paid to the logical relations of the thought-material; they ultimately find a veiled representation in the *formal* peculiarities of the dream. The effects of the dream-thoughts undergo slighter alterations than their conceptual content. As a rule, they are suppressed; where they are preserved, they are freed from the concepts and combined in accordance with their similarity. Only one part of the dream-work—the revision, variable in amount, which is effected by the partially awakened conscious thought—is at all consistent with the conception which the writers on the subject have endeavoured to extend to the whole performance of dream-formation.   *IoD—ch. 6*

Dream-Work and the Ego—With the help of the unconscious, every dream in the process of formation makes a demand upon the ego for the satisfaction of an instinct (if it originates from the id) or for the solution of a conflict, the removal of a doubt, or the making of a decision (if it originates from a residue of preconscious activity in waking life). The sleeping ego, however, is focused upon the wish to maintain sleep; it regards this demand as a disturbance and seeks to get rid of the disturbance. The ego achieves this by what appears to be an act of compliance: it meets the demand with what is in the circumstances the innocent fulfillment of a wish and thus disposes of the demand. This replacement of a demand by the fulfilment of a wish remains the essential function of dream-work.   *OoPA—ch. 5*

DROPPING OF OBJECTS—As can sometimes be demonstrated by analysis, the dropping of objects or the overturning and breaking of the same, are very frequently utilized as the expression of unconscious streams of thought, but more often, they serve to represent the superstitious or odd significances connected therewith in popular sayings.   *PEL—ch. 8*

E

EATING—The most frequent disturbance of the nutritive function is anorexia through withdrawal of libido. Increased desire to eat is also not infrequent; there is also a compulsion to eat, motivated by a fear of starvation, which has been little studied. As an hysterical defense against eating, the symptom of vomiting is familiar. Refusal to eat as a reaction to anxiety belongs among the psychotic patterns of behavior (delusions of poisoning).   *PoA—ch. 1*

EDUCATION—*Education* can without further hesitation be described as an incitement to the conquest of the pleasure-principle, and to its replacement by the reality-principle.
                                                          FMPF

EGO—We recognize in man a psychical organization which is interpolated between his sensory stimuli and perception of his bodily needs on the one hand, and his motor activity on the other; and which mediates between them with a certain purpose. We call this organization his "I." [Ego]   *QLA—ch. 2*

The ego is the organized part of the id.   *PoA—ch. 3*

The ego is an organization; it is dependent on the free intercommunication of, and the possibility of reciprocal interplay between, all its constituent elements; its desexualized energy still gives evidence of its origin in its striving for union and unification, and this compulsion to synthesis increases in direct proportion to the strength which the ego attains.   *PoA—ch. 3*

The principal characteristics of the ego are these. In consequence of the relation which was already established between sensory perception and muscular action, the ego is in control of voluntary movement. It has the task of self-preservation. As regards *external* events, it performs that task by becoming aware of the stimuli from without, by storing up experiences of them (in the memory), by avoiding excessive stimuli (through flight), by dealing with moderate stimuli (through adaptation) and, finally, by learning to bring about appropriate modifications in the external world to its own advantage (through activity). As regards *internal* events, in relation to the id, it performs that task by gaining control over the demands of the instincts, by deciding whether they shall be allowed to obtain satisfaction, by postponing that satisfaction to times and circumstances favorable in the external world or by suppressing their excitations completely. Its activities are governed by considerations of the tensions produced by stimuli present within it or introduced into it. The raising of these tensions is in general felt as *unpleasure* and their lowering as *pleasure*. It is probable, however, that what is felt as pleasure or unpleasure is not the *absolute* degree of the tensions, but something in the rhythm of their changes. The ego pursues pleasure and seeks to avoid unpleasure. An increase in unpleasure which is expected and foreseen is met by a *signal of anxiety;* the occasion of this increase, whether it threatens from without or within, is called a danger. From time to time the ego gives up its connection with the external world and withdraws into the state of sleep, in which its organization undergoes far-reaching changes. It may be inferred from the state of sleep that that organization consists in a particular distribution of mental energy.

OoPA—ch. 1

. . . The ego owes its origin as well as the most important of its acquired characteristics to its relation to the real external world; and we are thus prepared to assume that the pathological states of the ego—in which it most approximates once again the id—are founded upon a cessation or slackening of that relation to the external world.   *OoPA—ch. 8*

The ego is principally determined by the individual's own experience, that is to say by accidental and current events.

OoPA—ch. 1

The severest demand upon the ego is probably the keeping down of the instinctual claims of the id, and for this end the ego is obliged to maintain great expenditures of energy upon anti-cathexes. But the claims made by the super-ego, too, may become so powerful and so remorseless that the ego may be crippled, as it were, for its other tasks.   *OoPA—ch. 6*

No such purpose as that of keeping itself alive or of protecting itself from dangers by means of anxiety can be attributed to the id. That is the business of the ego, which is also

concerned with discovering the most favorable and least peril-
ous method of obtaining satisfaction, taking the external
world into account. *OoPA—ch. 2*

The *ego* was developed out of the cortical layer of the id,
which, being adapted for the reception and exclusion of stimuli,
is in direct contact with the external world. Its psychological
function consists in raising the processes in the id to a higher
dynamic level (perhaps by transforming freely mobile into
bound energy, such as corresponds to the preconscious condition); its constructive function consists in interposing, between
the demand made by an instinct and the action that satisfies it,
an intellective activity which, after considering the present state
of things and weighing up earlier experiences, endeavors by
means of experimental actions to calculate the consequences of
the proposed line of conduct. *OoPA—ch. 8*

Ego, Split in the—The ego can take itself as object, it
can treat itself like any other object, observe itself, criticize
itself, and do Heaven knows what besides with itself. In such a
case one part of the ego stands over against the other. The ego
can, then, be split; it splits when it performs many of its functions, at least for the time being. The parts can afterwards join
up again. *NILP—ch. 3*

The view which postulates that in all psychoses there is a
split in the ego could not demand so much notice, if it were not
for the fact that it turns out to apply also to other conditions
more like the neuroses and, finally, to the neuroses themselves.
OoPA—ch. 8

EGO AND ITS RELATIONSHIP TO CONSCIOUSNESS—
The processes in the Ego (they alone) *may* become conscious.
But they are not all conscious, nor always so, nor necessarily
so; and large parts of the Ego may remain unconscious indefi-
nitely. *QLA—ch. 2*

EGO AND ITS RELATIONSHIP TO THE ID—Under the
influence of the real external world which surrounds us, one
portion of the id has undergone a special development. From
what was originally a cortical layer, provided with organs for
receiving stimuli and with apparatus for protection against
excessive stimulation, a special organization has arisen which
henceforward acts as an intermediary between the id and the
external world. This region of our mental life has been given
the name of *ego*. *OoPA—ch. 1*

. . . In several points the Ego and the Id differ sharply from each other. Psychical acts issue in the Ego under other rules than those which apply in the Id; the Ego pursues different ends, and by different means.   *QLA—ch. 2*

The ego represents what we call reason and sanity, in contrast to the id which contains the passions.   *E & I—ch. 2*

In the Id there are no conflicts; contradictions and antitheses exist side by side, and often equalize matters between themselves by compromise formations. But the Ego, in similar case, feels a conflict which must be decided, and the decision consists in giving up one impulse in favor of the other. The Ego is an organization, marked out by a very noteworthy tendency toward unity and synthesis; the Id has not this character—it is, so to speak, all in pieces, and its individual impulses pursue their ends independently and regardless of one another.
    QLA—ch. 2

[The] instincts fill the Id; to put it shortly, all energy in the ID comes from them. The forces in the Ego, too, have no other origin, they are all derived from those in the Id. . . . The instincts in the Id press for immediate satisfaction, regardless of all else, and in this way either fail of achievement or actually do damage. It is the Ego's task to avert these mishaps, to mediate between the pretensions of the Id and preventions of the outer world.   *QLA—ch. 3*

There is no natural enmity between Ego and Id, they belong together and in a healthy case there is in practice no division between them. . . . So long as the Ego, and its connections with the Id, fulfill these ideal requirements there will be no neurotic disturbance.   *QLA—ch. 3*

The Id is the older; the Ego has developed out of it through the influence of the outer world as the bark develops around a tree. Our primary instincts start in the Id; all processes in the Id are unconscious. The Ego corresponds, as I have mentioned, with the realm of the preconscious; parts of it normally remain unconscious. The psychical processes in the "Id" obey quite different laws; their course and the influence they exert on one another are different from those that reign in the Ego. It is the discovery of these differences that has guided us to our new understanding and lends confirmation to it.

The repressed material must be regarded as belonging to the Id and obeys its mechanisms; it differs from it only in respect of its genesis. This differentiation takes place during the early period, when the Ego is developing out of the Id. Then the Ego takes possession of part of the Id and raises it to the preconscious level; other parts are thus not affected and remain in the Id as the "unconscious" proper. . . . As regards the passage between the two mental provinces we assume, on the one hand, that unconscious processes in the Id can be raised to a preconscious level and incorporated into the Ego, and, on the other hand, that preconscious material in the Ego can travel the opposite way and be shifted back into the Id.

M & M—Part III, Section I

One can hardly go wrong in regarding the ego as that part of the id which has been modified by its proximity to the external world and the influence that the latter has had on it, and which serves the purpose of receiving stimuli and protecting the organism from them, like the cortical layer with which a particle of living substance surrounds itself. This relation to the external world is decisive for the ego. . . . In popular language we may say that the ego stands for reason and circumspection, while the id stands for the untamed passions. *NILP—ch. 3*

On the whole the ego has to carry out the intentions of the id; it fulfils its duty if it succeeds in creating the conditions under which these intentions can best be fulfilled. One might compare the relation of the ego to the id with that between a rider and his horse. The ego has separated itself off from one part of the id by means of repression-resistances. But the barrier of repression does not extend into the id; so that the repressed material merges into the rest of the id.

NILP—ch. 3

EGO AND ITS RELATIONSHIP TO THE PRECONSCIOUS—The inside of the ego, which comprises above all the intellective processes, has the quality of being preconscious. This is characteristic of the ego and belongs to it alone.

OoPA—ch. 4

The Ego is essentially preconscious (virtually conscious), but parts of the Ego are unconscious.

M & M—Part III, Section I

EGO AND ITS RELATIONSHIP TO THE SUPEREGO—The relation of the ego to the superego: as regards many situations they are one and the same; as a rule we can distinguish them only when a state of tension, a conflict between them, has arisen. *PoA—ch. 3*

EGO AND ITS RELATIONSHIP TO THE UNCONSCIOUS —The Ego is essentially preconscious (virtually conscious), but parts of the Ego are unconscious.

M & M—Part III, Section I

EGO-ALTERATION, REACTIVE—See *Anticathexis in Hysteria.*

EGO-IDEAL—See *Superego.*

EGO-LIBIDO—We have laid down the concept of libido as a force of variable quantity by which processes and transformations in the spheres of sexual excitement can be measured. This libido we distinguished from the energy which is at the basis of the psychic processes in general as far as their special origin is concerned, and we thus attribute to it also a qualitative character. In separating libidinal from other psychic energy, we give expression to the assumption that the sexual processes of the organism are differentiated from the nutritional processes through a special chemism. The analyses of perversions and psychoneuroses have taught us that this sexual excitement is furnished not only from the so-called sexual parts alone, but from all organs of the body. We thus formulate for ourselves the concept of a *libido-quantum,* the psychic representative of which we designate as the *ego-libido.* The production, increase, distribution, and displacement of this ego-libido, thus offer the possible explanation for the manifest psychosexual phenomena.

But this ego-libido can only become conveniently accessible to psychoanalytic study if its psychic energy is invested or occupied (cathexis) in sexual objects; that is, if it becomes object-libido. We can then see it as it concentrates and fixes itself on objects, or as it leaves those objects and passes over to others, from which position it directs the individual's sexual activity; that is, as it leads to partial and temporary extinction of the libido. Psychoanalysis of the so-called transference neuroses (hysteria and compulsion neurosis) offers us here a reliable insight. *TCTS III*

[See also *Libido, Ego and Object.*]

EGO-RESISTANCE—The resistance which we have to overcome in analysis is produced by the ego, which clings tenaciously to its anticathexes. The ego finds it difficult to turn its attention to perceptions and ideas the avoidance of which it had until then made a rule, or to acknowledge as belonging to it impulses which constitute the most complete antithesis to those familiar to it as its own. Our combating of resistance in the analysis is based upon this conception of it. We make the resistance conscious where, as so often, in consequence of its connection with the repressed, it is unconscious; we oppose logical arguments to it when or after it has become conscious, promising the ego advantages and rewards if it renounces the resistance. As regards the resistance of the ego there is therefore nothing to call into question or to correct. On the other hand, the question is whether resistance alone covers the situation that confronts us in analysis. We experience the fact that the ego still finds it difficult to nullify its repressions even after it has resolved to give up its resistances, and we have designated the phase of strenuous effort which follows upon this laudable resolution as the period of "working through."

POA—ch. 11

EGO-SYNTONIC—In conformity with the ego.

NILP—ch. 1

ELECTRA COMPLEX—See *Oedipus complex; also Husband, Choice of.*

EROS—We have decided to assume the existence of only two basic instincts, *Eros* and the *destructive instinct.* (The contrast between the instincts of self-preservation and of the preservation of the species, as well as the contrast between ego-love and object-love, fall within the bounds of Eros.) The aim of the first of these basic instincts is to establish ever greater unities and to preserve them thus—in short, to bind together.

OoPA—ch. 2

EROTISM, ANAL—See *Anal Character.*

EROTOGENIC ZONES—The most prominent of the parts of the body from which this libido [which, from its instinctual aim, is known as sexual excitation] arises are described by the name of *erotogenic zones,* though strictly speaking the whole body is an erotogenic zone. *OoPA—ch. 2*

ERRORS IN ACTIONS—All cases [of lapses of our motor functions] in which the faulty effect seems to be the essential element—that is, the deviation from the intention—I denote as erroneously carried-out actions or defaults. *PEL—ch. 8*

ERRORS OF MEMORY—See *Memory, Errors of.*

ETHICS—Ethics must be regarded as a therapeutic effort: as an endeavour to achieve something through the standards imposed by the superego which had not been attained by the work of civilization in other ways.   *C & D—ch. 8*

We may say that a part of its [ethics] precepts is explained rationally by the necessity of marking off the rights of the community to the individual, those of the individual to the community, and those of individuals to one another. What, however, appears mysterious, grandiose, and mystically self-evident owes it character to its connection with religion, its origin in the will of the father.   *M & M—Part III, Section II*

EXCESS—Every excess carries within itself the seeds of its own surcease.   *PoA—ch. 5*

EXCRETA—Faeces are the child's first *gift*, the first sacrifice of his affection, a portion of his own body which he is ready to part with, but only for the sake of some one he loves.
     HIF—ch. 7

EXHIBITION-DREAM—See *Dreams, Exhibition in.*

EXHIBITIONISM—In the history of the childhood of neurotics exposure before children of the opposite sex plays a prominent part; in paranoia the delusion of being observed while dressing and undressing may be directly traced to these experiences; and among those who have remained perverse there is a class in whom the childish impulse is accentuated into a symptom: the class of *exhibitionists*.   *IoD—ch. 5*

EXPECTATION, ANXIOUS—Anxious expectation fades off imperceptibly into normal anxiousness. It comprises all that is covered by the word "nervousness"—apprehensiveness, the tendency to look on the dark side of things; but at every opportunity it exceeds the limits of this plausible form of nervousness and is frequently recognized by the patient himself as a kind of compulsion.   *A-N*

With regard to anxious expectation, clinical experience has taught us that there is a regular relationship between it and the disposition of the libido in the sexual life.   *NILP—ch. 4*

F

FALLING—To fall, to make a misstep, or to slip need not always be interpreted as an entirely accidental miscarriage of a motor action. The linguistic double meaning of these expressions points to diverse hidden phantasies, which may present themselves through the giving up of bodily equilibrium. I recall a number of lighter nervous ailments in women and girls which made their appearance after falling without injury, and which were conceived as traumatic hysteria as a result of the shock of the fall. At that time, I already entertained the impression that these conditions had a different connection, that the fall was already a preparation of the neurosis, and an expression of the same unconscious phantasies of sexual content which may be taken as the moving forces behind the symptoms.

PEL—ch. 8

[See also *Dreams of Falling*.]

FATHER, FATHER-FIXATION, etc.—See *Parents.*

FAULTY AND CHANCE ACTIONS—The common character of the mildest, as well as the severest cases, to which the faulty and chance actions contribute, lies *in the ability to refer the phenomena to unwelcome, repressed psychic material, which, though pushed away from consciousness, is nevertheless not robbed of all capacity to express itself. PEL—ch. 10*

FEAR—Fear requires a definite object of which one is afraid.
BPP—ch. 2

    Fear of Animals—See *Zoöphobia.*

    Fear of High Places—See also *Anxiety, Instinctual.*

FEELING—We also receive conscious information from the inside of the body—the feelings, which actually exercise a more peremptory influence upon our mental life than external perceptions; moreover, in certain circumstances the sense organs themselves transmit feelings, sensations of pain, in addition to the perceptions which are specific to them.

OoPA—ch. 4

FETISH, FETISHISM—This abnormality, which can be counted as one of the perversions, is, as is well known, based upon the patient, who is almost always male, not recognizing the fact that women have no penis—a fact which is exceedingly distasteful to him because of the evidence it affords of the possibility of his being castrated himself. He therefore rejects the perception of his own senses, which showed him that women's genitals lack a penis, and holds fast to the opposite conviction. The rejected perception, however, does not remain entirely without effects, for, in spite of everything, the patient has not the courage to assert that he really saw a penis. He snatches hold of something else instead—a part of the body or some other object—and attributes to it the rôle of the penis which he cannot do without. It is usually something that he actually saw at the moment at which he saw the woman's genitals, or it is something which can suitably serve as a symbolic substitute for the penis. Now it would not be right to describe this process which accompanies the formation of a fetish as a split in the ego; it is a compromise formed with the aid of displacement, such as we have been familiar with in dreams.

OoPA—ch. 8

See also *Sexual Object, Unfit Substitutes for.*

Fetish, Shoe and Foot as—The fetish-like reverence for the feminine foot and shoe seems to take the foot only as a substitutive symbol for the once revered and since then missed member of the woman. [Cf. *Castration Complex, Phallic Mother.*]

LDV—ch. 3

FIRE—I conjecture that, in order to possess himself of fire, it was necessary for man to renounce the homosexually-tinged desire to extinguish it by a stream of urine.

APF

FIXATION—Fixation can be described in this way. One instinct or instinctual component fails to accompany the rest along the anticipated normal path of development, and, in consequence of this inhibition in its development, it is left behind at a more infantile stage. The libidinal current in question then behaves in regard to later psychological structures as though it belonged to the system of the unconscious, as though it were repressed. [See also *Parents; Trauma, Fixation to the*.]

ParDP—ch. 3

FLYING—See *Dreams of Flying*.

FOETUS—Cf. *Birth and Anxiety*.

FORE-PLEASURE—The increment of pleasure which is offered us in order to release yet greater pleasure arising from deeper sources in the mind is called an "incitement premium" or technically, "fore-pleasure." *RPDD*

FORGETTING—The forgetting in all cases is proved to be founded on a motive of displeasure. *PEL—ch. 7*

The forgotten material is not extinguished, only "repressed"; its traces are extant in the memory in their original freshness, but they are isolated by "counter-cathexes." They cannot establish contact with the other intellectual processes; they are unconscious, inaccessible to consciousness.

M & M—Part III, Section I

No person forgets to carry out actions that seem important to himself without exposing himself to the suspicion that he is suffering from some mental disturbance. . . . I have collected the cases of neglect through forgetting which I have observed in myself, and endeavored to explain them. In doing so, I have found that they could invariably be traced to some interference of unknown and unadmitted motives—or, as may be said, they were due to a *counter-will*. . . . Cases in which we forget to carry out actions which we have promised to do as a favor for others, can similarly be explained as antagonism to conventional duty and as an unfavorable inward opinion.

PEL—ch. 7

Forgetting of Dreams—Often enough it happens that, however much he may try, the patient cannot remember one of his dreams. But when, by a piece of analytical work, we have removed a difficulty which has been disturbing the patient in his relation to the analysis, the forgotten dream will come into his mind quite suddenly. *NILP—ch. 1*

Forgetting, Mechanism of—I can perhaps give the following outline concerning the mechanism of actual forgetting. The memory material succumbs in general to two influences, condensation and distortion. Distortion is the work of the tendencies dominating the psychic life and directs itself above all against the affective remnants of memory traces which maintain a more resistive attitude towards condensation. The traces which have grown indifferent, merge into a process of condensation without opposition; in addition, it may be observed that tendencies of distortion also feed on the indifferent material, because they have not been gratified where they wished to manifest themselves. As these processes of condensation and distortion continue for long periods, during which all fresh experiences act upon the transformation of the memory content, it is our belief that it is time that makes memory uncertain and indistinct. It is quite probable that in forgetting, there can really be no question of a direct function of time. From the repressed memory traces, it can be verified that they suffer no changes even in the longest periods. The unconscious, at all events, knows no time limit. The most important, as well as the most peculiar character of psychic fixation consists in the fact that all impressions are, on the one hand, retained in the same form as they were received, and also in the forms that they have assumed in their further development. This state of affairs cannot be elucidated by any comparison from any other sphere. By virtue of this theory, every former state of the memory content may thus be restored, even though all original relations have long been replaced by newer ones.

PEL—ch. 10

Forgetting, Motivated—Painful memories merge into motivated forgetting with special ease.   *PEL—ch. 7*

Forgetting of Names—I was led to examine exhaustively the phenomenon of temporary forgetfulness through the observation of certain peculiarities, which, although not general, can, nevertheless, be seen clearly in some cases. In these, there is not only *forgetfulness*, but also false *recollection;* he who strives for the escaped name brings to consciousness others— substitutive names—which, although immediately recognized as false, nevertheless obtrude themselves with great tenacity. The process which should lead to the reproduction of the lost name is, as it were, displaced, and thus brings one to an incorrect substitute.

Now it is my assumption that the displacement is not left to psychic arbitrariness, but that it follows lawful and rational paths. In other words, I assume that the substitutive name (or names) stands in direct relation to the lost name, and I hope, if I succeed in demonstrating this connection, to throw light on the origin of the forgetting of names. . . . When we recapitulate the conditions for forgetting a name with faulty recollection we find: (1) a certain disposition to forget the name; (2) a process of suppression which has taken place shortly before; and (3) the possibility of establishing an *outer* association between the concerned name and the element previously suppressed. The last condition will probably not have to be much overrated, for the slighest claim on the association is apt in most cases to bring it about. But it is a different and farther-reaching question whether such outer association can really furnish the proper condition to enable the suppressed element to disturb the reproduction of the desired name, or whether after all a more intimate connection between the two themes is not necessarily required. On superficial consideration, one may be willing to reject the latter requirement and consider the temporal meeting in perfectly dissimilar contents as sufficient. But on more thorough examination, one finds more and more frequently that the two elements (the repressed and the new one) connected by an outer association, possess besides a connection in content. . . . I believe that one is not justified in separating the cases of name-forgetting with faulty recollection from those in which incorrect substitutive names have not obtruded themselves. . . . Besides the simple forgetting of proper names, there is another forgetting which is motivated by repression.   *PEL—ch. 1*

The mechanism of forgetting, or rather of losing or temporary forgetting of a name, consists in the disturbance of the intended reproduction of the name through a strange stream of thought unconscious at the time. Between the disturbed name and the disturbing complex, there exists a connection either from the beginning or such a connection has been formed—perhaps by artificial means—through superficial (outer) associations.

The self-reference complex (personal, family or professional) proves to be the most effective of the disturbing complexes. . . . To avoid the awakening of pain through memory is one of the objects among the motives of these disturbances.

In general, one may distinguish two principal cases of name-forgetting; when the name itself touches something unpleasant, or when it is brought into connection with other associations which are influenced by such effects. Thus, names can be disturbed on their own account or on account of their nearer or more remote associative relations in the reproduction.

A review of these general principles readily convinces us

that the temporary forgetting of a name is observed as the most frequent faulty action of our mental functions.

However, we are far from having described all the peculiarities of this phenomenon. I also wish to call attention to the fact that name-forgetting is extremely contagious. In a conversation between two persons, the mere mention of having forgotten this or that name by one often suffices to induce the same memory slip in the other. But wherever the forgetting is induced, the sought-for name easily comes to the surface.

There is also a continuous forgetting of names in which whole chains of names are withdrawn from memory. If, in the course of endeavoring to discover an escaped name, one finds others with which the latter is intimately connected, it often happens that these new names also escape. The forgetting thus jumps from one name to another, as if to demonstrate the existence of a hindrance not to be easily removed.   *PEL—ch. 3*

In the case of forgetting names, *we are aware* that the substitutive names are *incorrect*.   *PEL—ch. 4*

FORTUNE-TELLERS—During the psycho-analytic treatment of patients I have had the impression that the activities of professional fortune-tellers provide an admirable opportunity for making really satisfactory observations of thought-transference.   *NILP—ch. 2*

FRIENDSHIP—Aim-inhibited love [leads] to [the forming of] "friendships."   *C & D—ch. 4*

FRIGIDITY, SEXUAL—The sexual frigidity of women is a phenomenon which is insufficiently understood. Sometimes it is psychogenic, and, if so, it is accessible to influence; but in other cases one is led to assume that it is constitutionally conditioned or even partly caused by an anatomical factor.   *NILP—ch. 5*

FRIGHT—Fright is the name of the condition to which one is reduced if one encounters a danger without being prepared for it; it lays stress on the element of surprise.   *BPP—ch. 2*

FRUSTRATION—The most immediate, most easily discerned, and most comprehensible exciting cause of the onset of neurotic illness lies in that external factor which may generally be described as *frustration*. The person was healthy as long as his erotic need was satisfied by an actual object in the outer world; he becomes neurotic as soon as he is deprived of this object and no substitute is forthcoming. Happiness here coincides with health, unhappiness with neurosis.   *TNN*

G

GENITAL—Cf. *Sexuality*.

GOD [cf. also DEITIES]—The doctrine is that the universe was created by a being similar to man, but greater in every respect, in power, wisdom, and strength of passion, in fact by an idealized superman. . . . It is interesting to notice that this creator of the universe is always a single god, even when many gods are believed in. Equally interesting is the fact that the creator is nearly always a male, although there is no lack of indication of the existence of female deities and many mythologies make the creation of the world begin precisely with a male god triumphing over a female goddess, who is degraded into a monster. This raises the most fascinating minor problems, but we must hurry on. The rest of our enquiry is made easy because this God-Creator is openly called Father. Psychoanalysis concludes that he really is the father, clothed in the grandeur in which he once appeared to the small child. The religious man's picture of the creation of the universe is the same as his picture of his own creation. . . . He therefore looks back to the memory-image of the overrated father of his childhood, exalts it into a Deity, and brings it into the present and into reality. The emotional strength of this memory-image and the lasting nature of his need for protection are the two supports of his belief in God.   *NILP—ch. 7*

GRIEF—Grief is the reaction specific to object loss.
PoA—ch. 11

GROUP—An individual in a group is subjected through its influence to what is often a profound alteration in his mental activity.   *GPAE—ch. 4*

GUILT

  Guilt, Consciousness of—[See *Sense of Guilt and Consciousness.*]

69

Guilt Feeling—We know of two sources for feeling of guilt: that arising from the dread of authority and the later one from the dread of the super-ego. The first one compels us to renounce instinctual gratification; the other presses over and above this towards punishment, since the persistence of forbidden wishes cannot be concealed from the super-ego.

C & D—ch. 7

Guilt, Sense of—The tension between the strict super-ego and the subordinate ego we call the sense of guilt; it manifests itself as the need for punishment.   *C & D—ch. 7*

Our moral sense of guilt is the expression of the tension between the ego and the super-ego.   *NILP—ch. 3*

The sense of inferiority and the sense of guilt are exceedingly difficult to distinguish.   *NILP—ch. 3*

We cannot disregard the conclusion that man's sense of guilt has its origin in the Oedipus complex and was acquired when the father was killed by the association of the brothers.

C & D—ch. 7

. . . The sense of guilt or consciousness of guilt, as it is called in disregard of the fact that the patient does not feel it and is not aware of it . . . is evidently the portion of the resistance contributed by a superego that has grown peculiarly severe and cruel. The patient must not be healthy, he must remain ill, for he deserves no better. . . . The sense of guilt also offers an explanation of the cure or improvement of severe neuroses which we sometimes observe after real accidents: all that matters is that the patient should be wretched—in what way is of no consequence. . . . In dealing with this resistance we are obliged to restrict ourselves to making it conscious and attempting the gradual demolition of the hostile superego.

OoPA—ch. 6

Guilt, Sense of (in Analysis)—As far as the patient is concerned this sense of guilt is dumb; it does not tell him he is guilty; he does not feel guilty, he simply feels ill. This sense of guilt expresses itself only as a resistance to recovery which it is extremely difficult to overcome.   *E & I—ch. 5*

Guilt, Sense of (in Religion)—"Unconscious guilt" represents the resistance from the Super-Ego.   *QLA—ch. 5*

The different religions have never overlooked the part played by the sense of guilt in civilization. What is more, they come forward with a claim . . ., to save mankind from this sense of guilt, which they call sin.

C & D—ch. 8

Guilt, Unconscious Sense of—See *Punishment, Unconscious Need for*.

H

HAPPINESS—What is called happiness in its narrowest sense comes from the satisfaction—most often instantaneous—of pent-up needs which have reached great intensity, and by its very nature can only be a transitory experience.

C & D—ch. 2

HATE—It is noteworthy that in the use of the word "hate" no such intimate relation to sexual pleasure and the sexual function appears [as in "love"]: on the contrary, the painful character of the relation seems to be the sole decisive feature.

I & V

HELPLESSNESS, PSYCHIC—Psychic helplessness is the danger which is consonant with the period of immaturity of the ego, as object loss is the danger appertaining to the state of dependence of early childhood, the danger of castration to the phallic phase, and dread of the superego to the latency period.

PoA—ch. 8

HERMAPHRODITISM—Science shows cases in which the sexual characteristics appear blurred so that the sexual distinction is difficult, especially on an anatomical basis. The genitals of such persons unite the male and female characteristics (hermaphroditism). In rare cases both parts of the sexual apparatus are well developed (true hermaphroditism), but usually both are stunted.

TCTS I

In both sexes the degree of physical hermaphroditism is to a great extent independent of the psychical hermaphroditism.

PHW

HERO-WORSHIP—The great majority of people have a strong need for authority which they can admire, to which they can submit, and which dominates and sometimes even ill-treats them. We have learned from the psychology of the individual whence comes this need of the masses. It is the long-

72

ing for the father that lives in each of us from his childhood days, for the same father whom the hero of legend boasts of having overcome. *M & M—Part III, Section II*

HOMOSEXUALITY—Analysis shows that in every case a homosexual attachment to an object has at one time been present and in most cases has persisted in a latent condition. *OoPA—ch. 3*

Homosexuals are persons who, owing to the erotogenic importance of their own genitals, cannot do without a similar feature in their sexual object. In the course of their development from auto-erotism to object-love, they have remained at a point of fixation between the two.

There is absolutely no justification for distinguishing a special homosexual instinct. What constitutes a homesexual is a peculiarity not in his instinctual life but in his object-choice.

Cf. Castration Complex.

Homosexuals, Male—Homosexual men who have started in our times an energetic action against the legal restrictions of their sexual activity are fond of representing themselves through theoretical spokesmen as evincing a sexual variation, which may be distinguished from the very beginning, as an intermediate stage of sex or as "a third sex." In other words, they maintain that they are men who are forced by organic determinants originating in the germ to find that pleasure in the man which they cannot feel in the woman. As much as one would wish to subscribe to their demands out of humane considerations, one must nevertheless exercise reserve regarding their theories which were formulated without regard for the psychogenesis of homosexuality. . . . In all our male homosexuals there was a very intensive erotic attachment to a feminine person, as a rule to the mother, which was manifest in the very first period of childhood and later entirely forgotten by the individual. This attachment was produced or favored by too much love from the mother herself, but was also furthered by the retirement or absence of the father during the childhood period. . . . Following this primary stage, a transformation takes place whose mechanisms we know but whose motive forces we have not yet grasped. The love of the mother cannot continue to develop consciously so that it merges into repression. The boy represses the love for the mother by putting himself in her place, by identifying himself with her, and by taking his own person as a model through the similarity of which he is guided in the selection of his love object. He thus becomes homosexual; as a matter of fact, he returns to the stage of autoerotism, for the boys whom the growing adult now loves are only substitutive persons or revivals of his own childish person, whom he loves in the same way as his mother loved him. We say that he finds his love object on the road to narcissism, for the Greek legend called a boy Narcissus to whom nothing was more pleasing than his own mirrored image, and who became transformed into a beautiful flower of this name.

Deeper psychological discussions justify the assertion that the person who becomes homosexual in this manner remains fixed in his unconscious on the memory picture of his mother. By repressing the love for his mother he conserves the same in his unconscious and henceforth remains faithful to her. When as a lover he seems to pursue boys, he really thus runs away from women who could cause him to become disloyal to his mother.   *LDV—ch. 3*

HUMOR—Humor is not resigned; it is rebellious. It signifies the triumph not only of the ego, but also of the pleasure principle, which is strong enough to assert itself here in the face of the adverse real circumstances.   *Hum*

HUSBAND, CHOICE OF—In females, we find that it is the effect of their lack of a penis that drives them into their Œdipus complex. It does little harm to a woman if she remains in her feminine Œdipus attitude. (The name of "Electra complex" has been proposed for it.) She will in that case choose her husband for his paternal characteristics and will be ready to recognize his authority.   *OoPA—ch. 7*

HYPNOID STATE—Peculiar dream-like states of consciousness with diminished capacity for association.   *DNP*

HYPNOSIS—Hypnosis is a case rather different from that of analysis. It is the inducement of an abnormal mental state, and at the present day is only employed, by laymen, for purpose of entertainment.   *QLA—ch. 6*

HYPOCHONDRIA—Hypochondria, like organic disease, manifests itself in distressing and painful bodily sensations and also concurs with organic disease in its effect upon the distribution of the libido.   *Narc*

HYSTERIA—*A passive sexual experience before puberty:* this is the specific ætiology of hysteria. [Cf. *Anxiety-Hysteria*.]

Hysteria, Conversion—Many of the conversion hysterias of childhood are not carried over into later life.   *PoA—ch. 9*

Hysteria, Reaction Formation in—In hysteria a certain amount of ego-alteration through reaction formation is evident, in many circumstances becoming so striking that it claims attention as the cardinal symptom of the clinical syndrome. In this manner, for example, the ambivalency conflict in hysteria is resolved; hate for a loved person is kept submerged by an excess of tenderness towards him and of anxious concern about him. . . . The reaction formation of hysteria adheres tenaciously to a specific object and is not elevated to the status of a general disposition of the ego.   *PoA—ch. 11*

Hysteria, Traumatic—In regard to traumatic hysteria it is obviously the accident which has evoked the syndrome.
PMHP—ch. 1

Hysterical Attack—The hysterical attack is an equivalent of coitus.   *GRHA*

The regular and essential content of a (recurrent) hysterical attack is the recurrence of a psychical state which the patient has experienced earlier, in other words, the recurrence of a *memory*.   *THA*

If one would explain the hysterical seizure, one needs only, indeed, to look for the situation in which the movements in question were part of the behavior appropriate to that situation.
PoA—ch. 8

Hysterical Blindness—The hysterical blind are blind in consciousness only, while in the unconscious they are sighted.
PVD

Hysterical Identification—See *Identification in Hysteria*.

Hysterical Imitation—The ability of hysterical subjects to imitate all the symptoms which impress them when they occur in others, as though pity were aroused to the point of reproduction.   *IoD—ch. 4*

Hysterical Paralysis—Hysterical paralysis shows an *exact delimitation* and an *excessive intensity*.   *CSOHP*

I maintain that the lesion in hysterical paralyses must be entirely independent of the anatomy of the nervous system, since *hysteria behaves in its paralyses and other manifestations as if anatomy were non-existent, or as if it had no knowledge of it.*   *CSOHP*

Hysterical Symptoms—A hysterical symptom is based upon phantasy instead of upon the repetition of real experience.   *GPAE—ch. 2*

Hysterical Symptoms and Wish-Fulfillment—A hysterical symptom originates only where two contrary wish-fulfillments, having their source in different psychic systems, are able to meet in a single expression.   *IoD*

I

ID—To the oldest of the mental provinces or agencies we give the name of *id*. It contains everything that is inherited, that is present at birth, that is fixed in the constitution—above all, therefore, the instincts, which originate in the somatic organization and which find their first mental expression in the id in forms unknown to us.   *OoPA—ch. 1*

You must not expect me to tell you much that is new about the id, except its name. It is the obscure inaccessible part of our personality; the little we know about it we have learnt from the study of dream-work and the formation of neurotic symptoms, and most of that is of a negative character, and can only be described as being all that the ego is not. We can come nearer to the id with images, and call it a chaos, a cauldron of seething excitement. We suppose that it is somewhere in direct contact with somatic processes, and takes over from them instinctual needs and gives them mental expression, but we cannot say in what substratum this contact is made. These instincts fill it with energy, but it has no organization and no unified will, only an impulse to obtain satisfaction for the instinctual needs, in accordance with the pleasure-principle. The laws of logic—above all, the law of contradiction—do not hold for processes in the id. Contradictory impulses exist side by side without neutralizing each other or drawing apart; at most they combine in compromise formations under the overpowering economic pressure towards discharging their energy. There is nothing in the id which can be compared to negation, and we are astonished to find in it an exception to the philosophers' assertion that space and time are necessary forms of our mental acts. In the id there is nothing corresponding to the idea of time, no recognition of the passage of time, and (a thing which is very remarkable and awaits adequate attention in philosophic thought) no alteration of mental processes by the passage of time. . . . Naturally, the id knows no values, no good and evil, no morality. . . . Instinctual cathexes seeking discharge,—that, in our view, is all that the id contains.   *NILP—ch. 3*

The power of the id expresses the true purpose of the individual organism's life. This consists in the satisfaction of its innate needs. No such purpose as that of keeping itself alive or of protecting itself from dangers by means of anxiety can be attributed to the id. That is the business of the ego. . . .
                                          OoPA—ch. 2

In the Id there are no conflicts; contradictions and antitheses exist side by side, and often equalize matters between themselves by compromise formations.   *QLA—ch. 2*

. . . Everything which goes on in the Id is unconscious and remains so. . . .   *QLA—ch. 2*

The id cannot be afraid, as the ego can; it is not an organization, and cannot estimate situations of danger.   *PoA—ch. 8*

The core of our being, then, is formed by the obscure *id,* which has no direct relations with the external world and is accessible even to our own knowledge only through the medium of another agency of the mind. . . . The id, which is cut off from the external world, has its own world of perception. . . . The id obeys the inexorable pleasure principle.
                                          OoPA—ch. 8

See also *Ego and Its Relationship to the Id.*

Id and Ego—See *Ego and Its Relationship to the Id.*

Id and Unconscious—The sole quality that rules in the id is that of being unconscious. Id and unconscious are as intimately united as ego and preconscious; indeed, the former connection is even more exclusive. If we look back at the developmental history of the individual and of his psychical apparatus, we shall be able to make an important distinction in the id. Originally, of course, everything was id; the ego was developed out of the id by the continual influence of the external world. In the course of this slow development certain material in the id was transformed into the preconscious condition and was thus taken into the ego. Other material remained unaltered in the id, as its hardly accessible nucleus. But during this development the young and feeble ego dropped and pushed back into the unconscious condition certain material which it had already taken in, and behaved similarly in regard to many new impressions which it *might* have taken in, so that these were rejected and were able to leave traces in the id only. In consideration of its origin, we term this portion of the id *the repressed.*   *OoPA—ch. 4*

IDEAS, CONSCIOUS, PRECONSCIOUS AND UNCON-SCIOUS—We realize that what distinguishes a conscious idea from a preconscious one, and this from an unconscious one, cannot be anything but a modification, or perhaps also another distribution, of psychic energy. We speak of cathexes and hypercathexes, but beyond this we lack all knowledge and even a beginning for a useful working hypothesis.

M & M—Part III, Section I

IDEAS, DESIRED AND UNDESIRED—On falling asleep the "undesired ideas" emerge, owing to the slackening of a certain arbitrary (and, of course, also critical) action, which is allowed to influence the trend of our ideas; we are accustomed to speak of fatigue as the reason of this slackening; the emerging undesired ideas are changed into visual and auditory images. In the condition which is utilized for the analysis of dreams and pathological ideas, this activity is purposely and deliberately renounced, and the psychic energy thus saved (or some part of it) is employed in attentively tracking the undesired thoughts which now come to the surface—thoughts which retain their identity as ideas (in which the condition differs from the state of falling asleep). *"Undesired ideas" are thus changed into "desired" ones.* . . . The "undesired ideas" habitually evoke the most violent resistance, which seeks to prevent them from coming to the surface.

IoD—ch. 2

IDENTIFICATION—First, identification is the original form of emotional tie with an object; secondly, in a regressive way it becomes a substitute for a libidinal object tie, as it were by means of the introjection of the object into the ego; and thirdly, it may arise with every new perception of a common quality shared with some other person who is not an object of the sexual instinct.   *GPAE—ch. 7*

One ego becomes like another, one which results in the first ego behaving itself in certain respects in the same way as the second; it imitates it, and as it were takes it into itself. This identification has been not inappropriately compared with the oral cannibalistic incorporation of another person.

NILP—ch. 3

Identification in Hysteria—In hysteria identification is most frequently employed to express a sexual community. The hysterical woman identifies herself by her symptoms most readily—though not exclusively—with persons with whom she has had sexual relations, or who have had sexual intercourse with the same persons as herself. Language takes cognizance of this tendency: two lovers are said to be "one." In hysterical phantasy, as well as in dreams, identification may ensue if one simply thinks of sexual relations; they need not necessarily become actual. *IoD—ch. 4*

Identification and Object-Choice—Identification is a very important kind of relationship with another person, probably the most primitive, and is not to be confused with object-choice. One can express the difference between them in this way: when a boy identifies himself with his father, he wants to *be like* his father; when he makes him the object of his choice, he wants to *have* him, to possess him; in the first case his ego is altered on the model of his father, in the second case that is not necessary. Identification and object-choice are broadly speaking independent of each other; but one can identify oneself with a person, and alter one's ego accordingly, and take the same person as one's sexual object. It is said that this influencing of the ego by the sexual object takes place very often with women, and is characteristic of femininity. . . . If one has lost a love-object or has had to give it up, one often compensates oneself by identifying oneself with it; one sets it up again inside one's ego, so that in this case object-choice regresses, as it were, to identification. *NILP—ch. 3*

ILLNESS

Illness, Advantage Gained by—Illness may be used as a protection—to palliate incapacity at work or among competitors, or in family life as a means to force sacrifices and demonstrations of affection from others, or impose one's will upon them. All this is comparatively on the surface, and we put it all together under the heading "advantage gained by illness"; the only remarkable thing is that the patient—his Ego—knows nothing of the whole connection of such motives with his resulting behavior. *QLA—ch. 5*

Illness as Self-Punishment—It is very important for mental health that the Super-Ego should develop normally—that is, that it should become sufficiently depersonalized. It is precisely this that does not happen in the case of a neurotic, because his Œdipus complex does not undergo the right transformation. His Super-Ego deals with his Ego like a strict father with a child, and his idea of morality displays itself in primitive ways by making the Ego to submit to punishment by the Super-Ego. Illness is employed as a means for this "self-punishment." The neurotic has to behave as though he were mastered by guilt, which the illness serves to punish, and so to relieve him.

QLA—ch. 5

Illness as Protection—See *Illness, Advantage Gained by.*

IMPOTENCE, PSYCHIC—The sexual function is subject to a great multiplicity of disturbances, the majority of which have the character of simple inhibitions. These are grouped together as psychic impotence. *PoA—ch. 1*

Here again—as very probably in all neurotic disorders—the root of the trouble lies in an arrest occurring during the course of development of the libido to that ultimate form which may be called normal. [Cf. also *Castration-Anxiety*.]

CPL-DEL

INCUBATION PERIOD (OF TRAUMATIC NEUROSES)—The phenomenon of a latency in the neurosis between the first reactions to the trauma and the later appearance of the illness must be recognized as typical. *M & M—Part III, Section I*

The time that elapsed between the accident and the first appearance of the symptoms is called the "incubation period," a transparent allusion to the pathology of infectious disease. . . .

M & M—Part III, Section I

INDIVIDUAL PSYCHOLOGY—In reality Individual Psychology has very little to do with analysis, but, for certain historical reasons, lives a sort of parasitic existence at its expense. . . . The name itself is unsuitable, and seems to be a product of embarrassment; we cannot assent to any interference with its correct application as meaning the opposite of Group Psychology; for the matter of that our own concern is, first and foremost, the psychology of the human individual.

NILP—ch. 6

INFERIORITY

"**Inferiority Complex**"—As a matter of fact the phrase "inferiority-complex" is hardly ever used in psycho-analysis. It does not refer to anything which we regard as simple, let alone elementary.   *NILP—ch. 3*

Inferiority, Sense of—To trace it back to the perception in oneself of some organic disability or other, as the school of so-called Individual Psychologists like to do, seems to us a short-sighted error. The sense of inferiority has a strong erotic basis. The child feels itself inferior when it perceives that it is not loved, and so does the adult as well. The only organ that is really regarded as inferior is the stunted penis—the girl's clitoris. But the major part of the sense of inferiority springs from the relationship of the ego to its super-ego, and, like the sense of guilt, it is an expression of the tension between them. The sense of inferiority and the sense of guilt are exceedingly difficult to distinguish. Perhaps we should do better if we regarded the former as the erotic complement to the sense of moral inferiority.   *NILP—ch. 3*

INHIBITION—Inhibition is the expression of a *functional limitation of the ego*—a limitation which may have a large variety of causes.   *PoA—ch. 1*

One may say of inhibitions, in fine, that they represent a limitation and restriction of ego functions, either precautionary or resulting from an impoverishment of energy.   *PoA—ch. 1*

The more general inhibitions of the ego follow a simple mechanism. When the ego is occupied with a psychic task of special difficulty, as for example by mourning, a wholesale suppression of affect, or by the necessity for holding constantly mounting sexual fantasies in check, it becomes so impoverished with respect to the energy available to it that it is driven to restrict its expenditure in many places at the same time like a speculator who has tied up his money in his various enterprises.
                                                      PoA—ch. 1

Inhibition and Anxiety—Many inhibitions are an obvious renunciation of function, because the exercise of the function would give rise to anxiety.   *PoA—ch. 1*

Inhibition, Occupational—Inhibition in the field of occupation, which so often becomes a matter of treatment as an isolated symptom, is evidenced in diminished pleasure in work, or in its poor execution, or in such reactive manifestations as fatigue (vertigo, vomiting) if the subject forces himself to go on working. Hysteria compels the suspension of work by producing paralysis of organs and functions, the existence of which is incompatible with the carrying on of work. The compulsion neurosis interferes with work by a continuous distraction of the attention and by loss of time in the form of procrastination and repetition. [Certain] inhibitions evidently subserve a desire for self-punishment, as for example not infrequently those in the sphere of vocational activity. The ego dares not do certain things because they would bring an advantage and a success which the strict superego has forbidden. Thereupon the ego renounces these activities also, *in order not to become involved in conflict with the superego.*

PoA—ch. 1

Inhibition, Specific—In the case of certain particular inhibitions the trend expressed is rather easily recognized. When playing the piano, writing, and even walking are made the subject of neurotic inhibition, analysis reveals as the basis thereof an excessive erotization of the organ involved in the function in question, the fingers and the feet. (Cf. also *Walking, Writing.*)

PoA—ch. 1

Inhibition vs. Symptom—It is easy to see wherein an inhibition differs from a symptom. A symptom can no longer be described as a process taking place either in or around the ego.

PoA—ch. 1

The two concepts are not rooted in the same soil. Inhibition relates specifically to function and does not necessarily denote something pathological; a normal restriction or reduction of a function may also be termed an inhibition of it. To speak of a symptom, on the other hand, is tantamount to indicating a morbid process. Thus an inhibition may also be a symptom. Our habits of speech are such, then, as cause us to speak of an inhibition when a simple reduction of function is present, of a symptom when it is a question of an unusual alteration of function or of a new modality thereof. In many cases it seems to be perfectly arbitrary whether one emphasizes the positive or the negative aspect of a pathological process, whether one terms its result a symptom or an inhibition.

PoA—ch. 1

INSTINCT—The forces which we assume to exist behind the

tensions caused by the needs of the id are called *instincts*. They represent the somatic demands upon mental life. Though they are the ultimate cause of all activity, they are by nature conservative; the state, whatever it may be, which a living thing has reached, gives rise to a tendency to re-establish that state so soon as it has been abandoned. It is possible to distinguish an indeterminate number of instincts and in common practice this is in fact done. For us, however, the important question arises whether we may not be able to derive all of these various instincts from a few fundamental ones. We have found that instincts can change their aim (by displacement) and also that they can replace one another—the energy of one instinct passing over to another. This latter process is still insufficiently understood. After long doubts and vacillations we have decided to assume the existence of only two basic instincts. [See *Instincts, Basic*.]   *OoPA—ch. 2*

Instinct in general is regarded as a kind of elasticity of living things, an impulsion towards the restoration of a situation which once existed but was brought to an end by some external disturbance.   *ABS—ch. 5*

An instinct differs from a stimulus in that it arises from sources of stimulation within the body, operates as a constant force, and is such that the subject cannot escape from it by flight as he can from an external stimulus. An instinct may be described as having a source, an object and an aim. The source is a state of excitation within the body, and its aim is to remove that excitation; in the course of its path from its source to the attainment of its aim the instinct becomes operative mentally.   *NILP—ch. 4*

Observation shows us that an instinct may undergo the following vicissitudes: reversal into its opposite, turning round upon the subject, repression, sublimation.   *I & V*

By the *impetus* of an instinct we understand its motor element, the amount of force or the measure of the demand upon energy which it represents.

The *aim* of an instinct is in every instance satisfaction, which can only be obtained by abolishing the condition of stimulation in the source of the instinct.

The *object* of an instinct is that in or through which it can achieve its aim.

By the *source* of an instinct is meant that somatic process in an organ or part of the body from which there results a stimulus represented in mental life by an instinct.   *I & V*

Instinct of Aggression—Fortunately the instincts of aggression are never alone, they are always alloyed with the erotic ones.   *OoPA—ch. 2*

Instincts, Basic—After long doubts and vacillations we have decided to assume the existence of only two basic instincts, *Eros* and the *destructive instinct*.

OoPA—ch. 2

There can be no question of restricting one or the other of the basic instincts to a single region of the mind. They are necessarily present everywhere. We may picture an initial state of things by supposing that the whole available energy of Eros, to which we shall henceforward give the name of *libido,* is present in the as yet undifferentiated ego-id and serves to neutralize the destructive impulses which are simultaneously present. (There is no term analogous to "libido" for describing the energy of the destructive instinct.)   *OoPA—ch. 2*

Instinct, Death; Instinct, Destructive—See *Death Instinct*.

Instinct of the Preservation of the Species—See *Eros*.

Instinct of Self-Preservation—See *Eros*.

Instinct, Sexual—The sexual instincts are remarkable for their plasticity, for the facility with which they can change their aims, for their interchangeability—for the ease with which they can substitute one form of gratification for another, and for the way in which they can be held in suspense, as has been so well illustrated by the aim-inhibited instincts.

NILP—ch. 4

Instinctual Demands as Traumas—Instinctual demands from within operate as "traumas" no less than excitations from the external world, especially if they are met halfway by certain dispositions.   *CoPA—ch. 7*

Instinctual Renunciation—See *Renunciation, Instinctual*.

Instinctual Situation—Frightening *instinctual* situations can in the last resort be traced back to *external* situations of danger.   *NILP—ch. 4*

INTENTION—An intention is an impulse for an action which

has already found approbation, but whose execution is post-
poned for a suitable occasion.   *PEL—ch. 7*

INTOXICATION—The crudest of the methods of influencing
the body, but also the most effective, is the chemical one: that
of intoxication . . . The services rendered by intoxicating sub-
stances in the struggle for happiness and in warding off misery
rank so highly as a benefit that both individuals and races have
given them an established position within their libido-economy.
It is not merely the immediate gain in pleasure which one owes
to them, but also a measure of that independence of the outer
world which is so sorely craved.   *C & D—ch. 2*

INVERSION, INVERT—There are men for whom the sexual
object is not woman but man, and there are women for whom
it is not man but woman. Such *persons* are designated as contrary sexuals, or better, inverts, and the situation of such a
relationship is called inversion. The number of such individuals is considerable, although it is difficult to estimate
them accurately. . . . *Conception of Inversion.* The first studies
of the inversion gave rise to the assumption that it was a sign
of innate nervous degeneration. This harmonized with the fact
that physicians first observed it among nervous persons, or
among those giving such an impression. There are two elements
which should be considered independently in this characterization: the congenitality, and the degeneration. . . . *Explanation of Inversions.* The nature of inversion is explained
neither by the assumption that it is congenital nor that it is
acquired. In the first case, we need to be told what there is in
it of the congenital, unless we are satisfied with the roughest
explanation, namely, that a person brings along a congenital
sexual instinct connected with a definite sexual object. In the
second case it is a question whether the manifold accidental
influences suffice to explain the acquisition, unless there is
something in the individual to meet it half way. The negation
of this last factor is inadmissible according to our former
conclusions. . . . *The Sexual Aim of the Invert.* The important fact to bear in mind is that no uniformity of the
sexual aim can be attributed to inversion. Intercourse *per
anum* in men by no means goes with inversion; masturbation
is just as frequently the exclusive aim; and the limitation of
the sexual aim to mere effusion of feelings is here even more
frequent than in heterosexual love. In women, too, the sexual
aims of the inverts are manifold, among which contact with

the mucous membrane of the mouth seems to be preferred.
TCTS 1

IRRITABILITY—An increase of irritability always signifies an accumulation of excitation or an inability to tolerate such an accumulation, that is, an absolute or a relative accumulation of excitation.   *A-N*

ISOLATION—A technique peculiar to compulsion neurosis, is that of *isolation*. Its reference is likewise to the motor sphere; and it consists in the interposition, after an unpleasant experience, as also after some act of the subject's own which is of significance in the sense of his neurosis, of a refractory period in which nothing more is allowed to happen, no perception registered, and no action performed. This at first sight strange behavior soon betrays its relation to repression. The effect of this isolation is the same, as in repression with amnesia. The isolation phenomena of compulsion neurosis reproduce this technique, but intensified by motor means and with a magic intent motor isolation is to furnish a guaranty of the interruption of coherence in thinking.   *PoA—ch. 6*

J

JEALOUSY—Jealousy is one of those affective states, like grief, that may be described as normal. If anyone appears to be without it, the inference is justified that it has undergone severe repression and consequently plays all the greater part in his unconscious mental life. The instances of abnormally intense jealousy met with in analytic work reveal themselves as constructed of three layers. The three layers or stages of jealousy may be described as (1) *competitive* or normal, (2) *projected*, and (3) *delusional* jealousy.   NM-JPH

L

LAPSUS LINGUAE—See *Slip of the Tongue.*

LATENCY PERIOD, SEXUAL—The period of life from the end of the fourth year to the first manifestations of puberty at about eleven.   *C & AE*

LAUGHTER—Thus, according to our assumption, the conditions for laughter are such that a sum of psychic energy hitherto employed in the cathexis of some paths may experience free discharge. And since not all laughter (but surely the laughter of wit), is a sign of pleasure, we shall be inclined to refer this pleasure to the release of previously existing cathetic energy.   *WRU—ch. V*

LAY ANALYST—Analytical training certainly intersects the circle of medical training, but it does not comprise it nor is it comprised within it.   *QLA—ch. 7*

The preparation for analytical practice is no simple and easy matter; the work is hard and the responsibility heavy. But, anyone who has undergone such a discipline, has been analyzed, has grasped the psychology of the unconscious as it is known today, has become versed in the scientific aspects of sexuality, and has learned the delicate technique of psychoanalysis, the art of interpretation, the way to combat resistances, and to manage the transference—*that person is no longer a layman in the field of psychoanalysis.*   *QLA—ch. 5*

So far as the patient is concerned, it does not matter whether the analyst is a doctor or not, so long as the danger of a mistake as to his case is secured against by the prescribed medical opinion before the analysis begins, and, if required, during its course. For him, it is incomparably more important that the analyst should possess such personal qualities as will command his confidence, and that he should have acquired the knowledge and insight, and the experience, which alone can fit him for his task.   *QLA—ch. 7*

Lay analysts, as they are found practicing today, are not chance-comers, recruited and trained without discrimination, but persons of academic standing.   *QLA—ch. 7*

LIBIDO—Libido is a term used in the theory of the instincts for describing the dynamic manifestation of sexuality.   *LT*

It is difficult to say anything of the behavior of the libido in the id and in the superego. Everything that we know about it relates to the ego, in which the whole available amount of libido is at first stored up. We call this state of things absolute, primary *narcissism*. It continues until the ego begins to cathect the presentations of objects with libido—to change narcissistic libido into *object libido*.   *OoPA—ch. 2*

Libido participates in every instinctual manifestation, but not everything in that manifestation is libido. Cf also *Instincts, Basic; Sexual Instinct and Libido*.   *C & D—ch. 6*

Libido, Ego and Object—We must understand that the ego is always the main reservoir of libido, from which libidinal cathexes of objects proceed, and into which they return again, while the greater part of this libido remains perpetually in the ego. There is therefore a constant transformation of ego-libido into object-libido, and of object-libido into ego-libido. But if this is so the two cannot differ from each other in their nature, and there is no point in distinguishing the energy of the one from that of the other; one can either drop the term "libido" altogether, or use it as meaning the same as psychic energy in general.   *NILP—ch. 4*

[See also *Ego-Libido*.]

Libido, Mobility of—A characteristic of libido which is important in life is its *mobility*, the ease with which it passes from one object to another. This must be contrasted with the *fixation* of libido to particular objects, which often persists through life.   *OoPa—ch.2*

Libido, Narcissistic—The Libido of the self-preservative instincts.   *LT*

Concerning the fates of the object-libido, we can also state that it may be withdrawn from the object, that it may be preserved in a floating state in special states of tension, and that it may finally be taken back into the ego and again change into ego-libido as *narcissistic libido*. Through psychoanalysis, we look as if over a boundary, which we are not permitted to pass, into the activity of this narcissistic libido, and thus, form an idea of relations between the two. The narcissistic or ego-libido appears to us as the great reservoir from which all object cathexis is sent out, and into which it is drawn back again, while the narcissistic libido-cathexis of the ego appears to us as the realized primal state in the first childhood, which only becomes hidden by the later emissions of libido, and is retained at the bottom behind them.   *TCTS III*

Libido, Object—See *Libido, Ego and Object*.

Libido, Somatic Sources of—There can be no question that the libido has somatic sources, that it streams into the ego from various organs and parts of the body. This is most clearly seen in the case of the portion of the libido which, from its instinctual aim is known as sexual excitation. The most prominent of the parts of the body from which this libido arises are described by the name of *erotogenic zones*, though strictly speaking the whole body is an erotogenic zone.   *OoPA—ch. 2*

LIBIDO-QUANTUM—See *Ego-Libido*.

LIES, CHILDREN'S—It is comprehensible that children should tell lies when in doing so they mimic the lies of grown-up people. But a number of the lies of well-brought-up children have a peculiar significance, and should cause their instructors to reflect rather than to be angry. These lies proceed from the influence of an excessive love motive.   *IML*

LITERATURE—I am of opinion that all the aesthetic pleasure we gain from the works of imaginative writers is of the same type as the "fore-pleasure," and that the true enjoyment of literature proceeds from the release of tensions in our minds.   *RPDD*

LOOKING, DESIRE FOR—The desire for looking becomes a perversion (a) when it is exclusively limited to the genitals; (b) when it becomes connected with the overcoming of loathing (voyeurs and onlookers at the functions of excretion); and (c) when instead of preparing for the normal sexual aim, it suppresses it.   *TCTS I*

LOVE—Love in itself, in the form of longing and deprivation, lowers the self-regard; whereas to be loved, to have love returned, and to possess the beloved object, exalts it again.   *Narc*

Being in love is based upon the simultaneous presence of directly sexual tendencies and of sexual tendencies that are inhibited in their aims, so that the object draws a part of the narcissistic ego-libido to itself. It is a condition in which there is only room for the ego and the object.   *GPAE—ch. 12*

Not to love before one gains full knowledge of the thing loved presupposes a delay which is harmful. When one finally reaches cognition, he neither loves nor hates properly; one remains beyond love and hatred. One has investigated instead of having loved.   *LDV—ch. 1*

Love, Sexual—One of the forms in which love manifests itself, sexual love, gives us our most intense experience of an overwhelming pleasurable sensation and so furnishes a proto-type for our strivings after happiness.   *C & D—ch. 2*

M

MAN—Let us venture to correct Trotter's pronouncement that man is a herd animal and assert that he is rather a horde animal, an individual creature in a horde led by a chief.

GPAE—ch. 9

MASOCHISM—Masochism comes under our observation in three shapes: as a condition under which sexual excitation may be roused; as an expression of feminine nature; and as a norm of behavior. According to this one may distinguish an *erotogenic, a feminine,* and a *moral* type of masochism. The first, the erotogenic masochism, the lust of pain, is also to be found at bottom in the other forms; the concept of it can be supported on biological and constitutional grounds; it remains incomprehensible unless one can bring oneself to make certain assumptions about matters that are wrapt in obscurity. The third, in certain respects the most important form in which masochism appears, has only lately, as a sense of guilt that is for the most part unconscious, been properly appreciated by psycho-analysis; it already admits, however, of full explanation and of co-ordination into our previous knowledge. Feminine masochism, on the other hand, is the form most accessible to observation, least mysterious, and is comprehensible in all its relations. *EPM*

Masochism and Femininity—We must not overlook one particularly constant relation between femininity and instinctual life. The repression of their aggressiveness, which is imposed upon women by their constitutions and by society, favours the development of strong masochistic impulses, which have the effect of binding erotically the destructive tendencies which have been turned inwards. Masochism is then, as they say, truly feminine. *NILP—ch. 5*

Masochism and Sadism—Masochism as a perversion seems further removed from the normal sexual goal than its

93

opposite [sadism]. It may even be doubted whether it ever is primary and whether it does not more often originate through transformation from sadism. It can often be recognized that masochism is nothing but a continuation of sadism directed against one's own person in which the latter at first takes the place of the sexual object. *TCTS I*

MASTURBATION—An overwhelming aetiological importance is attributed by neurotics to their masturbatory practices. They make them responsible for all their troubles, and we have the greatest difficulty in getting them to believe that they are wrong. But as a matter of fact we ought to admit that they are in the right, for masturbation is the executive agent of infantile sexuality, from the faulty development of which they are suffering. The difference is that what the neurotics are blaming is the masturbation of the pubertal stage: the infantile masturbation, which is the one that really matters, has for the most part been forgotten by them. *NILP—ch. 5*

Masturbation in Childhood—See *Sexuality in Childhood*.

MELANCHOLIA—Melancholia, or more accurately the melancholic attack. In this disease, about whose causes and mechanism we know far too little, the most remarkable characteristic is the way in which the superego—you may call it, but in a whisper, the conscience—treats the ego. The melancholiac during periods of health can, like any one else, be more or less severe towards himself; but when he has a melancholic attack, his super-ego becomes over-severe, abuses, humiliates, and ill-treats his unfortunate ego, threatens it with the severest punishments, reproaches it for long forgotten actions which were at the time regarded quite lightly, and behaves as though it had spent the whole interval in amassing complaints and was only waiting for its present increase in strength to bring them forward, and to condemn the ego on their account. The super-ego has the ego at its mercy and applies the most severe moral standards to it . . . after a certain number of months the whole moral fuss is at an end, the critical voice of the super-ego is silent, the ego is reinstated, and enjoys once more all the rights of man until the next attack. *NILP—ch. 3*

MEMORY—[Cf. also *Forgetting*.]

Memory, Concealed—See *Memory, Concealment of*.

Memory, Concealing—See *Memory, Concealment of*.

Memory, Concealment of—The formation of a concealing memory depends on the forgetting of other important impressions. In the case of forgetting of names, *we are aware* that the substitutive names are *incorrect,* while in concealing memories, we are surprised that we have them at all.

PEL—ch. 4

I particularly emphasized a peculiarity in the temporal relation between the concealing memory and the contents of the memory concealed by it. The content of the concealing memory in that example belonged to one of the first years of childhood, while the thoughts represented by it, which remained practically unconscious, belonged to a later period of the individual in question. I called this form of displacement a retro-active or *regressive* one. Perhaps more often, one finds the reversed relation—that is, an indifferent impression of the most remote period becomes a concealing memory in consciousness, which simply owes its existence to an association with an earlier experience, against whose direct reproduction there are resistances. We would call these *encroaching* or *interposing* concealing memories. What most concerns the memory lies here chronologically beyond the concealing memory. Finally, there may be a third possible case, namely, the concealing memory may be connected with the impression it conceals, not only through its contents, but also through contiguity of time; this is the *contemporaneous* or *contiguous* concealing memory.

PEL—ch. 4

Memory, Errors of—Errors of memory are distinguished from forgetting and false recollections through one feature only, namely, that the error (false recollection) is not recognized as such but finds credence. However, the use of the expression "error" seems to depend on still another condition. We speak of "erring" instead of "falsely recollecting" where the character of the objective reality is emphasized in the psychic material to be reproduced—that is, where something other than a fact of my own psychic life is to be remembered, or rather something that may be confirmed or refuted through the memory of others. The reverse of the error in memory in this sense is formed by ignorance. *PEL—ch. 10*

Memory, Visual—Some [adults] recall by means of visual pictures—their memories are of a visual character; other individuals can scarcely reproduce in memory the most paltry sketch of an experience; we call such persons *"auditifs"* and *"moteurs"* in contrast to the *"visuels,"* terms proposed by Charcot. These differences vanish in dreams; all our dreams are preponderatingly visual. But this development is also found in the childhood memories; the latter are plastic and visual, even in those people whose later memory lacks the visual element. The visual memory, therefore, preserves the type of the infantile recollections. Only my earliest childhood memories are of a visual character; they represent plastically depicted scenes, comparable only to stage settings.   *PEL—ch. 4*

MENTAL LIFE—Psychoanalysis makes a basic assumption. . . . We assume that mental life is the function of an apparatus to which we ascribe the characteristics of being extended in space and of being made up of several portions—which we imagine, that is, as being like a telescope or microscope or something of the sort.   *OoPA—ch. 1*

Our mental life as a whole is governed by *three polarities,* namely, the following antitheses: Subject (ego)—Object (external world), Pleasure—Pain, Active—Passive.   *I & V*

MENTAL PROCESSES—We have attributed three qualities to mental processes: they are either conscious, preconscious, or unconscious. The division between the three classes of material which have these qualities is neither absolute nor permanent.   *OoPA—ch. 4*

MILK—The complaint against the mother that harks back furthest, is that she has given the child too little milk, which is taken as indicating a lack of love. [Cf. also *Weaning.*]   *NILP—ch. 5*

MISTAKES—The effects which result from mistakes of normal persons are, as a rule, of a most harmless nature. Just for this reason, it would be particularly interesting to find out whether mistakes of considerable importance, which could be followed by serious results, as, for example, those of physicians or druggists, fall within the range of our point of view. . . . We can also add to these mistakes the case of one who gives a beggar a gold piece in place of a copper or a silver coin. The solution of such mishandling is simple: it is an act of sacrifice designed to mollify fate, to avert evil, and so on. If we hear a tender mother or an aunt express concern regarding the health of a child, immediately before taking a walk during which she displays her charity, contrary to her usual habit, we can hardly doubt the sense of this apparently undesirable accident. In this manner, our faulty acts make possible the practice of all those pious and superstitious customs which must shun the light of consciousness, because of the strivings against them of our unbelieving reason.   *PEL—ch. 8*

MODESTY—Modesty, which is regarded as a feminine characteristic *par excellence,* but is far more a matter of convention than one would think, was, in our opinion, originally designed to hide the deficiency in her genitals.   *NILP—ch. 5*

MORALITY—Morality, of course, does not develop simultaneously in all its departments, and furthermore, the duration of the amoral period of childhood differs in different individuals. Where this morality fails to develop we are prone to speak of "degeneration"; but here the case is obviously one of arrested development. Where the primary character is already overlaid by the later development it may be at least partially uncovered again by an attack of hysteria. The correspondence between the so-called hysterical character and that of a naughty child is positively striking. The obsessional neurosis, on the other hand, corresponds to a super-morality, which develops as a strong reinforcement against the primary character that is threatening to revive.   *IoD—ch. 5*

MORBID GAIN—See *Illness, Advantage Gained by.*

MOTHER, MOTHER-FIXATION, etc.—See *Parents.*

MOTILITY—Motility [manifests itself essentially] in actions designed to effect changes in the outer world.   *Ucs*

MOURNING—Mourning originates under the influence of reality testing, which demands categorically that one must part from the object because the object no longer exists. Now it is the task of mourning to carry out this retreat from the object in all the situations in which the object was the recipient of an intense cathexis. The painful character of this separation accords with the explanation just given—that is, it is explained by the intense and unrealizable longingful cathexis of the object during the reproduction of the situations in which the tie to the object has to be dissolved.   *PoA—ch. 11*

MOUTH, SEXUAL UTILIZATION OF—*Sexual Utilization of the Mucous Membrane of the Lips and Mouth.* The employment of the mouth as a sexual organ is considered as a perversion if the lips (tongue) of the one are brought into contact with the genitals of the other, but not when the mucous membrane of the lips of both touch each other. In the latter exception we find the connection with the normal.   *TCTS I*

MYSOGYNY—See *Castration Complex.*

N

NAKEDNESS—[Cf. *Clothing.*]

    Nakedness in Dreams—Dreams of nakedness are *exhibition-dreams.* [q.v.]　　　　　　　　　　　　　　*IoD—ch. 5*

NARCISSISM—The Greek legend called a boy Narcissus to whom nothing was more pleasing than his own mirrored image, and who became transformed into a beautiful flower of this name.　　　　　　　　　　　　　　　　　　　*LDV—ch. 3*

    [Cf. *Homosexuals, Male.*]

NEGATION—The subject-matter of a repressed image or thought can make its way into consciousness on condition that it is *denied*. Negation is a way of taking account of what is repressed; indeed, it is actually a removal of the repression, though not, of course, an acceptance of what is repressed.　*Neg*

NEGATIVISM OF PSYCHOTICS—The passion for universal negation, the "negativism" displayed by many psychotics, is probably to be regarded as a sign of a "defusion" of instincts due to the withdrawal of the libidinal components.　　*Neg*

NEURASTHENIA—On the one hand, we find cases in which definite symptoms characteristic of *neurasthenia* are conspicuous: cranial pressure, tendency to fatigue, dyspepsia, constipation, irritation of the spine, and so forth. On the other hand, in certain cases these indications are of minor importance and the syndrome is composed of other symptoms which all show a relation to one main symptom, to "anxiety" (free-floating anxiety, restlessness, expectant anxiety, complete, rudimentary or supplementary anxiety-attacks, locomotor vertigo, agoraphobia, sleeplessness, exacerbation of pains, etc.). I have left to the former type of neurasthenia its designation, but have distinguished the second as "anxiety-neurosis" both neuroses commonly appear together.　　　　　　　　　　　　　*SAoN*

NEUROSIS—Neurosis is the result of a conflict between the ego and its *id*.   *N & P*

The neurotic turns away from reality because he finds it unbearable—either the whole or parts of it.   *FPMF*

It is *quantitative disharmonies* that must be held responsible for the inadequacies and sufferings of neurotics. The determining causes of all the varying forms of human mental life are to be looked for in the interplay between inherited dispositions and accidental experiences.   *OoPA—ch. 7*

What did we regard as the essence of a neurosis? The fact that the Ego, the more highly organized part of the mental apparatus bred up under the influence of the outer world, is not in a position to fulfill its function of mediation between Id and reality; that in its weakness it retreats from some part of the instinctual activity of the Id; and suffers the consequences of this renunciation in the form of contractions of its influence, symptoms, and unsuccessful reaction-formations. *QLA—ch. 7*

Neurosis seems to be a human privilege.
                                        M & M—Part III, Section I

The neuroses have specific characteristics, they are misery of a particular sort.   *OoPA—ch. 7*

According to all that we know of the structure of the simpler neuroses of everyday life, it is very improbable that a neurosis should come about only by reason of the objective fact of exposure to danger without the participation of the deeper unconscious strata of the mental apparatus.   *PoA—ch. 7*

Defense against dangerous perceptions is a general task of neurosis.   *PoA—ch. 10*

It is indeed a universal characteristic of the neuroses that there are present in the subject's mental life, as regards some particular behavior, two different attitudes, contrary to each other and independent of each other; in that case, however, one of them belongs to the ego and the opposing one, which is repressed, belongs to the id.   *OoPA—ch. 8*

Neuroses, Actual—Neurasthenia and anxiety neurosis. . . . I am inclined to class hypochondria with neurasthenia and anxiety-neurosis as a third "actual neurosis."   *Narc*

Neurosis, Aetiology of—As a rule neuroses are *overdetermined;* that is to say, several factors in their aetiology operate together.   *RCA-N*

See *Neurosis, Formation of; Trauma, its Part in the Genesis of Neurosis.*

Neurosis, Anxiety—See *Anxiety, Neurotic; Anxiety-Neurosis.*

Neurosis, Childhood Influence in—See *Anxiety-Neurosis.*

The influence of childhood makes itself felt even in the situation at the beginning of the formation of a neurosis, since it plays a decisive part in determining whether and at what point the individual shall fail to master the real problems of life.
                                                        HIF—ch. 5

Neurosis in Childhood—Neuroses could be avoided if the child's sexual life were allowed free play, as happens among many primitive races.   *OoPA—ch. 8*

Since we came to see more clearly we have been tempted to say that childhood neurosis is not the exception but the rule; it is as though it were unavoidable in the passage from the infantile disposition to conformity with the culture achieved by society. In most cases, these neurotic spells of early years are overcome spontaneously; it may be that their traces are usually left even in those of average mental health.   *QLA—ch. 4*

It seems that neuroses are only acquired during early childhood (up to the age of six), even though their symptoms may not make their appearance until much later. The infantile neurosis may become manifest for a short time or may be overlooked. In every case the subsequent neurotic illness has this prelude in childhood as its point of departure. (It is possible that what are known as traumatic neuroses—brought about by excessive fright or severe somatic shocks such as railway collisions, explosions, etc.—are an exception; their relation to the infantile factor has hitherto eluded investigation.)
                                                        OoPA—ch. 7

A trauma in childhood can be immediately followed by a neurosis during childhood; this constitutes an effort of defense accompanied by the formation of symptoms. . . . A childhood neurosis seldom continues without an interval into the neurosis of the adult.   *M & M—Part III, Section I*

The neuroses of children, so far at least as concerns upper-class urban children of the white race, are regularly occurring episodes in development, although too little attention is still paid to them. In not a single adult neurotic do the indications of a childhood neurosis fail of occurrence, while on the other hand by no means all children who show them become neurotic subsequently.   *PoA—ch. 9*

Neurosis, Civilization and—We must not forget, therefore, to include the influence of civilization among the determinants of neuroses. It is easy, as we can see, for a barbarian to be healthy; for a civilized man the task is a hard one.
                                                            OoPA—ch. 7

Neurosis, Compulsion—See *Compulsion-Neurosis*.

Neurosis, Development of—Early trauma—defense—latency—outbreak of the neurosis—partial return of the repressed material: this was the formula we drew up for the development of a neurosis.   *M & M—Part III, Section I*

Neurosis, Formation of—As a consequence of a certain experience there arises an instinctual demand which claims satisfaction. The ego foregoes this satisfaction, either because it is paralyzed by the excessiveness of the demand or because it recognizes in it a danger. The first of these reasons is the original one; both end in the avoidance of a dangerous situation. The Ego guards against this danger by repression. The excitation becomes inhibited in one way or another; the incitement, with the observations and perceptions belonging to it, is forgotten. This, however, does not bring the process to an end; either the instinct has kept its strength, or it will regain it, or it is re-awakened by a new situation. It renews its claim and—since the way to normal satisfaction is barred by what we may call the scar tissue of repression—it gains at some weak point new access to a so-called substitutive satisfaction which now appears as a symptom, without the acquiescence and also without the comprehension of the Ego. All phenomena of symptom-formation can be fairly described as "the return of the repressed."   *M & M—Part III, Section II*

[Neurotic disturbance:] an Ego, prevented in its synthetizing activity, with no influence over a part of the Id, obliged to renounce some of its activities in order to avoid a fresh collision with what is repressed, exhausting itself in defense reactions—largely in vain—against the symptoms or derivatives of the repressed impulses; and an Id in which individual instincts have made themselves independent, pursuing their own aims without regard for the interests of the whole personality, and obeying only the laws of the primitive psychology which reigns in the depths of the Id. If we survey the whole situation it becomes clear that there is a simple formula for the arising of a neurosis; the Ego has made an attempt to suppress certain parts of the Id by an *inappropriate method,* and this has miscarried, and the Id has taken its revenge. Neurosis is thus the consequence of a conflict between Ego and Id, on which the Ego centers because—as further investigation shows—it insists throughout on retaining its adaptability towards the outer world. The opposition lies between outer world and Id, and because the Ego, true to its inmost nature, takes sides with the outer world, it becomes involved in conflict with its own Id. But mark well that it is not the fact of this conflict which brings about the illness—for such opposition between reality and Id is unavoidable, and the Ego's constant task is to mediate between them. It is the fact that the Ego, for settling the conflict, has employed the inadequate method of repression. But this in turn arises from the fact that at the time when this task was presented to it the Ego was undeveloped and weak. Decisive repressions all occur in early childhood. *QLA—ch. 3*

See also *Frustration; Trauma (Psychic) and the Formation of Neurosis.*

Neurosis, Infantile—See *Neurosis in Childhood.*

Neurosis and Internal Excitation—The nervous system reacts to an internal source of excitation with a neurosis, just as it reacts to an analogous external one with a corresponding affect. *A-N*

Neurosis and Normalcy—Neuroses (unlike infectious diseases, for instance) have no specific determinants. It would be idle to seek in them for a pathogenic factor. They shade off into what is described as the normal by a series of transitional steps; and on the other hand there is scarcely any condition generally recognized as normal in which it would not be possible to demonstrate neurotic traits. *OoPA—ch. 7*

Neurosis, Obsessional—The first symptoms of obsessional neurosis usually declare themselves in the second period of childhood (from six to eight years of age). [*Cf. Obsessive Acts and Ceremonials.*] *Pon.*

Neurosis, Origins of—If the relative weakness of the Ego is the determining factor for the occurrence of neurosis, it must also be possible that a later physical illness may produce a neurosis, if it in fact brings about a weakening of the Ego. And this is very often the case. A somatic disturbance may affect the instinctual activity in the Id, and increase the strength of the instincts beyond the limits to which the Ego is matched.
QLA—ch. 7

Neurosis and Perversion—A great part of the opposition to these, my theories, is explained by the fact that the sexuality from which I deduce the psychoneurotic symptoms is thought of as coincident with the normal sexual instinct. But psychoanalysis teaches us more than that. It shows that the symptoms do not by any means result at the expense only of the so-called normal sexual instinct (at least not exclusively or preponderately), but they represent the converted expression of impulses which in a broader sense might be designated as *perverse* if they could manifest themselves directly in phantasies and acts without deviating from consciousness. The symptoms are, therefore, partially formed at the cost of abnormal sexuality. *The neurosis is, so to say, the negative of the perversion.*
TCTS I

Neurosis and Psychosis—The neuroses and psychoses are states in which disturbances in the functioning of the [psychical] apparatus come to expression.   *OPA—ch. 7*

Neurosis is the result of a conflict between the ego and its id, whereas psychosis is the analogous outcome of a similar disturbance in the relation between the ego and its environment (outer world).   *N & P*

Neurosis and psychosis are clearly intimately related, and yet at a decisive point they must separate. This point might well be that at which the Ego decides which side it will take. In both cases the Id would stick to its character of blind obduracy.
QLA—ch. 3

Neurosis and Sex—Among the causes of and occasions for neurotic complaints sexual factors play an important, an over-weening—even perhaps a specific—rôle.   *QLA—ch. 4*

Neurosis, Symptoms of—See *Neurotic Symptoms*.

Neurosis, Traumatic—After severe shock of a mechanical nature, railway collision or other accident in which danger to life is involved, a condition may arise which has long been

recognized and to which the name "traumatic neurosis" is attached.
BPP—ch. 2

It may happen that someone gets away, apparently unharmed, from the spot where he has suffered a shocking accident, for instance a train collision. In the course of the following weeks, however, he develops a series of grave psychical and motor symptoms, which can be ascribed only to his shock or whatever else happened at the time of the accident. He has developed a "traumatic neurosis." . . . The time that elapsed between the accident and the first appearance of the symptoms is called the "incubation period," a transparent allusion to the pathology of infectious disease. *M & M—Part III, Section I*

In traumatic neurosis the active cause of the illness is not the trifling bodily injury but the affect of fright—the psychic trauma.
PMHP—ch. 1

In the experiences which result in traumatic neurosis the external protective mechanism against stimuli of excessive strength is broken down and excessive quanta of excitation gain access to the mental apparatus, so that here the second possibility exists that anxiety is not only employed as an affective signal but is also newly created in response to the economic demands of the situation. *PoA—ch. 7*

See also *Neurosis in Childhood; Trauma (Psychic) and the Formation of Neurosis.*

NEUROTIC SYMPTOMS—The symptoms of neuroses are exclusively, it might be said, either a substitutive satisfaction of some sexual impulse or measures to prevent such a satisfaction, and are as a rule compromises between the two, of the kind that arise according to the laws operating between contraries in the unconscious. *OoPa—ch. 7*

That a psychic process which develops anxiety may still be a wish-fulfilment has long ceased to imply any contradiction for us. We may explain this occurrence by the fact that the wish belongs to one system (the *Ucs.*), whereas the other system (the *Pcs.*) has rejected and suppressed it. The subjection of the *Ucs.* by the *Pcs.* is not thoroughgoing even in perfect psychic health; the extent of this suppression indicates the degree of our psychic normality. Neurotic symptoms indicate to us that the two systems are in mutual conflict; the symptoms are the result of a compromise in this conflict, and they temporarily put an end to it. On the one hand they afford the *Ucs.* a way out for the discharge of its excitation—they serve it as a kind of sally-gate—while, on the other hand, they give the *Pcs.* the possibility of dominating the *Ucs.* in some degree. It is instructive to consider, for example, the significance of a hysterical phobia, or of agoraphobia. A neurotic is said to be incapable of crossing the street alone, and this we should rightly call a "symptom." Let someone now remove this symptom by constraining him to this action which he deems himself incapable of performing. The result will be an attack of anxiety, just as an attack of anxiety in the street has often been the exciting cause of the establishment of an agoraphobia. We thus learn that the symptom has been constituted in order to prevent the anxiety from breaking out. The phobia is thrown up before the anxiety like a frontier fortress.   *IoD—ch. 7*

What features are common to all neurotic symptoms? Here we may note two important points. The effects of the trauma are twofold, positive and negative. The former are endeavours to revive the trauma, to remember the forgotten experience, or, better still, to make it real—to live through once more a repetition of it; if it was an early affective relationship it is revived in an analogous connection with another person. These endeavours are summed up in the terms "fixation to the trauma" and "repetition-compulsion." The effects can be incorporated into the so-called normal Ego and in the form of constant tendencies lend to it immutable character traits, although—or rather because—their real cause, their historical origin, has been forgotten. . . . . The negative reactions pursue the opposite aim; here nothing is to be remembered or repeated of the forgotten traumata. They may be grouped together as defensive reactions. They express themselves in avoiding issues, a tendency which may culminate in an inhibition or phobia. These negative reactions also contribute considerably to the formation of character. Actually they represent fixations on the trauma no less than do the positive reactions, but they follow the opposite tendency. The symptoms of the neurosis proper constitute a compromise, to which both the positive and negative effects of the trauma contribute; sometimes one component, sometimes the other, predominates. These opposite reactions create conflicts which the subject cannot as a rule resolve.
                              M & M—Part III, Section I

NEUROTICS—There is a class of psychological patients who evidently resemble the psychotics very closely, the immense number of sufferers from severe neuroses. The causes as well as the pathogenic mechanisms of their illness must be the same or at least very similar. Their ego, however, has proved more resistant and has become less disorganized. Many of them, in spite of their troubles and of their consequent inadequacy are none the less able to maintain their position in real life.

OoPa—ch. 6

There is no doubt that persons whom we call neurotic remain infantile in their attitude towards danger, and have not grown out of antiquated conditions for anxiety. Let us accept this as a factual contribution to our characterization of neurotics; why it should be so is not so easy to say. *NILP—ch. 4*

Neurotics have approximately the same innate dispositions as other people, they have the same experiences and they have the same problems to solve. *OoPA—ch. 7*

They complain of their illness, but they make the most of it, and when it comes to taking it away from them they will defend it like a lioness her young; there is no use in reproaching them with their contradiction. *QLA—ch. 5*

It is very important for mental health that the Super-Ego should develop normally—that is, that it should become sufficiently depersonalized. It is precisely this that does not happen in the case of a neurotic, because his Œdipus complex does not undergo the right transformation. His Super-Ego deals with his Ego like a strict father with a child, and his idea of morality displays itself in primitive ways by making the Ego submit to punishment by the Super-Ego. Illness is employed as a means for this "self-punishment." The neurotic has to behave as though he were mastered by guilt, which the illness serves to punish, and so to relieve him. *QLA—ch. 5*

NORMAL—[Neuroses] shade off into what is described as the normal by a series of transitional steps; and on the other hand there is scarcely any condition generally recognized as normal in which it would not be possible to demonstrate neurotic traits.

OoPA—ch. 7

Normal and Abnormal—The border-line between the nervous, normal and abnormal states is indistinct, and we are all slightly nervous. *PEL—ch. 10*

The distinction between what is psychologically normal and abnormal, in spite of its practical importance, possesses only a conventional value. *OoPA—ch. 8*

NUTRITIVE FUNCTION—See *Eating*.

O

OBJECT-CATHEXIS—The object-cathexes proceed from the instinctual demands of the id. *NILP—ch. 3*

OBJECT-CHOICE—See *Identification and Object-Choice.*

OBJECT-LIBIDO—See *Libido, Ego and Object.*

OBJECT-LOSS—Grief is basically the reaction specific to object loss, anxiety to the danger which this object loss entails, or, by a further displacement, to the danger of object loss itself. *PoA—ch. 11*

OBJECT, SEXUAL—See *Sexual Object.*

OBSESSION—Obsessions are always reproaches re-emerging in a transmuted form under repression—reproaches which invariably relate to a sexual deed performed with pleasure in childhood. *FRDNP*

Two components are found in every obsession: (1) an idea that forces itself upon the patient; (2) an associated emotional state. *O & P*

OBSESSIVE ACTS AND CEREMONIALS—The obsessive act serves to express *unconscious* motives and ideas. *OA & RL*

A sharp distinction between "obsessive acts" and "ceremonials" is not to be expected; as a rule an obsessive act develops from a ceremonial. *OA & RL*

A ceremonial begins as an act of defense or security—as a *protective measure.* *OA & RL*

The neurotic ceremonial consists of little prescriptions, performances, restrictions, and arrangements in certain activities of every-day life which have to be carried out always in the same or in a methodically varied way. *OA & RL*

OBSTINACY—See *Anal Character.*

OCCULT—Through the application of psycho-analytic theory, occult phenomena have been revealed which would otherwise have remained unrecognized.   *NILP—ch. 2*

ONANISM, SUPPRESSED—Just as every excess carries within itself the seeds of its own surcease, so this holds true too of compulsion neurosis, in that it is precisely the suppressed onanism which in the form of compulsive acts compels an ever furthered approximation to gratification.   *PoA—ch. 5*

OEDIPUS COMPLEX—*Œdipus complex,* so named because its essential substance is found in the Greek myth of King Œdipus, which has luckily been preserved for us in a version from the hand of a great dramatist. The Greek hero killed his father and married his mother. That he did so unknowingly, since he did not recognize them as his parents, constitutes a deviation from the analytical subject matter which is easily intelligible and indeed inevitable.   *OoPA—ch. 7*

Castration has a place, too, in the Œdipus legend, for the blinding with which Œdipus punished himself after the discovery of his crime is, by the evidence of dreams, a symbolic substitute for castration.   *OoPA—ch. 7*

Oedipus Complex in Women—With the transference of the child-penis wish on to her father, the girl enters into the situation of the Œdipus-complex. The hostility against her mother, which did not require to be newly created, now receives a great reinforcement, for her mother becomes a rival, who gets everything from her father that she herself wants. The girl's Œdipus-complex has long concealed from us the pre-œdipal attachment to her mother which is so important and which leaves behind it such lasting fixations. For the girl, the Œdipus situation is the conclusion of a long and difficult period of development, it is a kind of temporary solution of her problem, a state of equilibrium which is not lightly to be given up, especially as the onset of the latency period is not far off. And here we notice a difference between the two sexes in the relation between the Œdipus-complex and the castration-complex, a difference which is probably a momentous one. The boy's Œdipus-complex, in which he desires his mother, and wants to get rid of his father as a rival, develops naturally out of the phase of phallic sexuality. The threat of castration, however, forces him to give up this attitude. Under the influence of the danger of losing his penis, he abandons his Œdipus-complex; it is repressed and in the most normal cases entirely destroyed, while a severe super-ego is set up as its heir. What happens in the case of the girl is almost the opposite. The castration-complex prepares the way for the Œdipus-complex instead of destroying it; under the influence of her penis-envy the girl is driven from her attachment to her mother, and enters the Œdipus situation, as though it were a haven of refuge. When the fear of castration disappears, the primary motive is removed, which has forced the boy to overcome his Œdipus-complex. The girl remains in the Œdipus-situation for an indefinite-period, she only abandons it late in life, and then incompletely. The formation of the super-ego must suffer in these circumstances.   *NILP—ch. 5*

OEDIPUS LEGEND—In the very text of Sophocles' tragedy there is an unmistakable reference to the fact that the Œdipus legend had its source in dream-material of immemorial antiquity, the content of which was the painful disturbance of the child's relations to its parents caused by the first impulses of sexuality.   *IoD—ch. 5*

ORAL PHASE—The first of the *pre-genital phases* is called the *oral* phase.   *NILP—ch. 4*

The first organ to make its appearance as an erotogenic zone and to make libidinal demands upon the mind is, from the time of birth onward, the mouth. . . . Sadistic impulses already begin to occur sporadically during the oral phase along with the appearance of the teeth.   *OoPA—ch. 3*

ORDERLINESS—See *Anal Character.*

P

PAIN—Most of the "pain" we experience is of a perceptual order, perception either of the urge of unsatisfied instincts or of something in the external world which may be painful in itself or may arouse painful anticipations in the psychic apparatus and is recognized by it as "danger." *BPP—ch. 1*

    Pain, Physical—Pain—primarily and as a rule—occurs if a stimulus impinging on the periphery breaks through the defenses that oppose stimuli of excessive strength and hence acts like a continuous instinctual stimulus against which otherwise efficacious muscular activity such as serves to remove the stimulated region from the stimulus remains powerless. If the pain does not originate from a point on the skin but from an internal organ, this does not alter the situation in any way; it is only that a bit of the internal periphery has replaced the external. . . . In the case of physical pain there arises an intense cathexis, which may be termed narcissistic, of the painful region of the body—a cathexis which increases progressively and which acts upon the ego in a so to speak evacuative manner. *PoA—ch. 11*

    Pain, Psychic—It certainly cannot be without signficance that language has created the concept of inward, of psychic, pain, and has equated the sensations attendant upon object loss with physical pain. *PoA—ch. 11*

PANIC—A panic arises if a group of that kind becomes disintegrated. Its characteristics are that none of the orders given by superiors are any longer listened to, and that each individual is only solicitous on his own account, and without any consideration for the rest. The mutual ties have ceased to exist, and a gigantic and senseless dread is set free. *GPAE—ch. 5*

"PANSEXUALISM"—I have never maintained the assertion which has so often been ascribed to me that dream-interpretation shows that all dreams have a sexual content or are derived from sexual motive forces.   *ABS—ch. 4*

PARANOIA—On the basis of [certain] clinical evidence we can suppose that paranoiacs are endowed with a *fixation at the stage of narcissism,* and we can assert that the amount of *regression* characteristic of paranoia is indicated by the length of *the step back from sublimated homosexuality to narcissism.*
ParDP—ch. 3

Many things obtrude themselves on consciousness in paranoia, which in normal and neurotic persons can only be demonstrated through psychoanalysis as existing in their unconscious. (For example, the phantasies of the hysterical regarding sexual and cruel abuse which are made conscious by analysis often correspond in every detail with the complaints of persecuted paranoiacs. It is remarkable, but not altogether unexpected that we also meet the identical content as reality in the contrivances of perverts for the gratification of their desires.)   *PEL—ch. 10*

Paranoia, Projection in—The most striking characteristic of symptom-formation in paranoia is the process which deserves the name of *projection.* An internal perception is suppressed, and, instead, its content, after undergoing a certain degree of distortion, enters consciousness in the form of an external perception.   *ParDP—ch. 3*

Paranoia, Persecutory—In persecutory paranoia the sufferer takes a particular way of defending himself against an unduly strong homosexual attachment to a given person, with the result that the person he once loved most is changed into a persecutor and then becomes the object of aggressive and often dangerous impulses on the part of the patient. Here we have grounds for interposing an intermediate phase in which the love is transformed into hate.   *E & I—ch. 4*

PARAPHRENIA—It would seem to me the most convenient plan to give dementia praecox the name of *paraphrenia.* This term has no special connotation, and it would serve to indicate a relationship with paranoia (a name which may be regarded as fixed) and would further recall hebephrenia, an entity which is now merged in dementia praecox.   *ParDp—ch. 3*

Patients suffering from dementia praecox or schizophrenia whom I propose to term paraphrenics display two fundamental characteristics: They suffer from megalomania and they have withdrawn their interest from the external world (people and things).   *Narc*

The libido that is liberated by frustration does not remain attached to objects in phantasy, but returns to the ego; the megalomania then represents the mastery of this volume of libido, and thus corresponds with the introversion on to the phantasy-creations that is found in the transference neuroses; the hypochondria of paraphrenia, which is homologous to the anxiety of the transference neuroses, arises from a failure of this effort in the mental apparatus.   *Narc*

PARENTS—Cf. also *Superego*.

Parents as Love Objects—The first love-object of the boy is his mother, and she remains as such in the formation of his Œdipus- complex, and, ultimately, throughout his whole life. For the little girl, too, her mother must be her first object (together with figures of nurses and other attendants that merge into hers); the first object-cathexes, indeed, follow the lines of the satisfaction of the great and simple needs of life, and the circumstances in which the child is nursed are the same for both sexes. In the Œdipus situation, however, the father has become the little girl's love-object, and it is from him that, in the normal course of development, she should find her way to her ultimate object-choice. The girl has, then, in the course of time to change both her erotogenic zone and her object, while the boy keeps both of them unchanged.   *NILP—ch. 5*

Cf. also *Father-Fixation, Mother, Antagonism to*.

Parents, Sexual Wishes Toward—But no fact has more claim to our attention than this—that a small child's sexual wishes are regularly directed towards those who stand in closest relationship to it; in the first place, its father and mother, and beyond them its brothers and sisters. For a boy, the mother is the first love-object, for a girl the father, so far as a bisexual disposition does not call also for the reverse attitude at the same time. The other parent is felt to be a disturbing rival, and is not seldom regarded with acute enmity.   *QLA—ch. 4*

FATHER—I could not point to any need in childhood so strong as that for a father's protection.   *C & D—ch. 1*

The idea of being eaten by the father belongs to the typical primal stock of childhood ideas; analogies from mythology (Kronos) and from animal life are generally familiar.

PoA—ch. 4

Father-Fixation (in Women)—We have made the most surprising discoveries about these women who display intense and prolonged father-fixations. We knew, of course, that there had been an earlier stage in which they were attached to their mother; but we did not know that it was so rich in content, that it persisted so long, and that it could leave behind it so many occasions for fixations and predispositions. During this time, their father is no more than an irksome rival. In many cases the attachment to the mother lasts beyond the fourth year; almost everything that we find later in the father-relation was already present in that attachment, and has been subsequently transferred on to the father. In short, we gain the conviction that one cannot understand women, unless one estimates this *preoedipal attachment to the mother* at its proper value.

NILP—ch. 5

MOTHER—A child's first erotic object is the mother's breast that feeds him, and love in its beginnings attaches itself to the satisfaction of the need for food. To start with, the child certainly makes no distinction between the breast and his own body; when the breast has to be separated from his body and shifted to the "outside" because he so often finds it absent, it carries with it, now that it is an *"object,"* part of the original narcissistic cathexis. This first object subsequently becomes completed into the whole person of the child's mother, who not only feeds him but also looks after him and thus arouses in him many other physical sensations pleasant and unpleasant. By her care of the child's body she becomes his first seducer. In these two relations lies the root of a mother's importance, unique, without parallel, laid down unalterably for a whole lifetime, as the first and strongest love-object and as the prototype of all later love relations—for both sexes. The phylogenetic foundation has so much the upper hand in all this over accidental personal experience that it makes no difference whether a child has really sucked at the breast or has been brought up on the bottle and never enjoyed the tenderness of a mother's care. His development takes the same path in both cases; it may be that in the latter event his later longing is all the greater. And for however long a child is fed at his mother's breast, he will always be left with a conviction after he is weaned that his feeding was too short and too little.

OoPA—ch. 7

Phallic Mother—Important biological analogies have taught us that the psychic development of the individual is a short repetition of the course of development of the race, and we shall therefore not find improbable what the psychoanalytic investigation of the child's psyche asserts concerning the infantile estimation of the genitals. The infantile assumption of the maternal penis is thus the common source of origin for the androgynous formation of the maternal deities like the Egyptian goddess Mut.

LDV—ch. 3

Mother, Antagonism to (in Women)—[The] strong [preoedipal] attachment of the girl to her mother . . . is fated to give way to an attachment to her father. This step in development is not merely a question of a change of object. The turning away from the mother occurs in an atmosphere of antagonism; the attachment to the mother ends in hate. Such a hatred may be very marked and may persist throughout an entire lifetime; it may later on be carefully overcompensated; as a rule, one part of it is overcome, while another part persists. The outcome is naturally very strongly influenced by the actual events of later years. (Cf. also *Penis-Envy*.) *NILP—ch. 5*

Her love had as its object the phallic mother; with the discovery that the mother is castrated it becomes possible to drop her as a love-object, so that the incentives to hostility which have been so long accumulating, get the upper hand.

NILP—ch. 5

Mother-Identification (in Women)—The mother-identification of the woman can be seen to have two levels, the preoedipal, which is based on the tender attachment to the mother and which takes her as a model and the later one, derived from the Oedipus-complex, which tries to get rid of the mother and replace her in her relationship with the father. Much of both remains over for the future. *NILP—ch. 5*

PARSIMONIOUSNESS—See *Anal Character*.

PAST, LURE OF—Remote times have a great attraction—sometimes mysteriously so—for the imagination. As often as mankind is dissatisfied with its present—and that happens often enough—it harks back to the past and hopes at last to win belief in the never forgotten dream of a Golden Age. Probably man still stands under the magic spell of his childhood, which a not unbiased memory presents to him as a time of unalloyed bliss.   M & M—Part III, Section 1

PCPT-CS—Perceptual-conscious [q.v.]

PENIS-ENVY (PENIS-WISH)—A further characteristic of the sexuality of early childhood is that the female organ as yet plays no part in it—the child has not yet discovered it. All the accent falls on the male organ, and all interest is concentrated on whether it is present or not.   QLA—ch. 4

If we penetrate deeply into the neuroses of women, we not infrequently meet with the repressed wish to possess a penis. We call this infantile wish "penis-envy" and include it within the castration complex. . . .   TIAE

We ascribe a castration-complex to the female sex as well as to the male. That complex has not the same content in girls as in boys. The castration-complex in the girl, as well, is started by the sight of the genital organs of the other sex. She immediately notices the difference, and—it must be admitted—its significance. She feels herself at a great disadvantage, and often declares that she would "like to have something like that too," and falls a victim to *penis-envy*, which leaves ineradicable traces on her development and character-formation, and, even in the most favorable instances, is not overcome without a great expenditure of mental energy. That the girl recognizes the fact that she lacks a penis, does not mean that she accepts its absence lightly. On the contrary, she clings for a long time to the desire to get something like it, and believes in that possibility for an extraordinary number of years; and even at a time when her knowledge of reality has long since led her to abandon the fulfilment of this desire as being quite unattainable, analysis proves that it still persists in the unconscious, and retains a considerable charge of energy. . . . The discovery of her castration is a turning-point in the life of the girl. Three lines of development diverge from it; one leads to sexual inhibition or to neurosis, the second to a modification of character in the sense of masculinity complex, and the third to normal femininity. . . . At first the girl looks on her castration as a personal misfortune, and only gradually extends it to other females, and eventually to her mother.   NILP—ch. 5

The small girl feels sensitive over the lack of a sex organ

equal to the boy's, and holds herself to be inferior on that account; and that this "penis-envy" gives rise to a whole series of characteristic feminine reactions.   *QLA—ch. 4*

The girl holds her mother responsible for her lack of a penis, and never forgives her for that deficiency. [Cf. *Modesty; Parents (Phallic Mother)*.]   *NILP—ch. 5*

Child-Penis-Wish—The wish with which the girl turns to her father is, no doubt, ultimately the wish for the penis, which her mother has refused her and which she now expects from her father. The feminine situation is, however, only established when the wish for the penis is replaced by the wish for a child —the child taking the place of the penis, in accordance with the old symbolic equation. . . . Her happiness is great indeed when this desire for a child one day finds real fulfilment; but especially is this so if the child is a little boy who brings the longed-for penis with him.   *NILP—ch. 5*

PERCEPTION—All perceptions which come about through painful, tactile, and auditory, or visual stimuli are the more likely to be conscious.   *M & M—Part III, Section I*

Perceptions—All perceptions which are received from without *(sense-perceptions)* and from within—what we call sensations and feelings—are Cs from the start.
    E & I—ch. 2

Perception, Internal—Internal perceptions yield sensations of processes arising in the most diverse and certainly also in the deepest strata of the mental apparatus.
    E & I—ch. 2

PERCEPTUAL-CONSCIOUS SYSTEM—This systm is directed on to the external world, it mediates perceptions of it, and in it is generated, while it is functioning, the phenomenon of consciousness. It is the sense-organ of the whole apparatus, receptive, moreover, not only of excitations from without but also of such as proceed from the interior of the mind.
    NILP—ch. 3

PERVERSION—We have been forced to perceive in every fixed aberration from the normal sexual life, a fragment of inhibited development and infantilism. . . . The perversions thus prove themselves to be, on the one hand, inhibitions, and on the other, dissociations from the normal development.
    TCTS III

The union of the genitals in the characteristic act of copulation is taken as the normal sexual aim. . . . Yet, even in the most normal sexual act, certain addenda are distinguishable, the development of which may lead to aberrations described as *perversions*. . . . The perversions represent either (a) anatomical *transgressions* of the bodily regions destined for sexual union, or (b) a *lingering* at the intermediary relations to the sexual object which should normally be rapidly passed, on the way to the definite sexual aim.   *TCTS I*

See also *Neurosis and Perversion*.

Sadism and Masochism as Perversions—We use the word "sadism" when sexual satisfaction depends upon the sexual object suffering pain, ill-treatment and humiliation, and the word "masochism," when the subject himself has to suffer such treatment. You know, too, that there is a certain admixture of these two tendencies in normal sexual relations, and that we call them "perversions" when they thrust the other sexual aims into the background, and substitute their own aims for them.   *NILP—ch. 4*

PERVERT—There are people whose desires behave in every way like sexual ones, but who at the same time entirely disregard the sexual organs or their normal use; people of this kind are known as "perverts."   *OoPA—ch. 3*

PHALLIC MOTHER—See *Parents*.

PHALLIC PHASE—In the phallic phase there are the first signs of an organization which subordinates the other trends to the primacy of the genitals and signifies the beginning of a co-ordination of the general persuit of pleasure into the sexual function.   *OoPA—ch. 3*

This is, as it were, a forerunner of the final shape of sexual life, and already greatly resembles it. It is to be noted that what comes in question at this stage is not the genitals of both sexes but only those of the male (the phallus). The female genitals long remain unknown: in the child's attempt at understanding sexual processes, he pays homage to the venerable cloacal theory—a theory which has a genetic justification.
                              OoPA—ch. 3

Phallic Phase in Girls—We may assume that, in the phallic phase of the girl, the clitoris is the dominant erotogenic zone.

But it is not destined to remain so; with the change to femininity, the clitoris must give up to the vagina its sensitivity, and, with it, its importance, either wholly or in part.

NILP—ch. 5

[*Cf. Pregenital Phases.*]

PHALLIC PRIMACY PERIOD—While the child is at the highest point of its infantile sexual development, a genital organization of a sort is established; but only the male genitals play a part in it, and the female ones remain undiscovered. I have described this as the period of *phallic* primacy.

ABS—ch. 3

PHANTASY—Our phantasy always works on existing patterns. *QLA—ch. 7*

PHOBIA—We have in the phobias, after all, merely the substituting of one external danger for another. The fact that in phobias the ego is able to escape anxiety through a process of avoidance or by means of an inhibition is in complete accord with the concept that this anxiety is simply an affective signal, and that with regard to the economic situation involved nothing has been altered. *PoA—ch. 7*

Among the phobias two groups may be differentiated, according to the nature of the object feared: (1) common phobias, an exaggerated fear of all those things that everyone detests or fears to some extent: such as night, solitude, death, illness, dangers in general, snakes, etc.; (2) specific phobias, the fear of special circumstances that inspire no fear in the normal man; for example, agoraphobia and the other phobias of locomotion. *O & P*

Phobias of Early Childhood—The enigmatic phobias of early childhood deserve mention once again. Certain of them —the fear of being alone, of the dark, of strangers—we can understand as reactions to the danger of object loss; with regard to others—fear of small animals, thunderstorms, etc. —there is the possibility that they represent the atrophied remnants of an innate preparedness against reality dangers such as is so well developed in other animals. It is the part of this archaic heritage having to do with object loss which alone has utility for man. If such childhood phobias become fixed, grow more intense, and persist into a later period of life, analysis demonstrates that their content has become connected with instinctual demands, has become the representative of internal dangers also.   *PoA—ch. 11*

Phobia and Sexual Life—The main point in the problem of phobias seems to me that *phobias do not occur at all when the vita sexualis is normal.*   *RCA-N*

PLEASURE AND UNPLEASURE—The ego's activities are governed by consideration of the tensions produced by stimuli present within it or introduced into it. The raising of these tensions is in general felt as *unpleasure* and their lowering as *pleasure.*   *OoPA—ch. 1*

PLEASURE PRINCIPLE (PLEASURE-PAIN PRINCIPLE) —In the psycho-analytical theory of the mind we take it for granted that the course of mental processes is automatically regulated by "the pleasure-principle": that is to say, we believe that any given process originates in an unpleasant state of tension and thereupon determines for itself such a path that its ultimate issue coincides with a relaxation of this tension, i.e. with avoidance of "pain" or with production of pleasure.
                                    BPP—ch. 1

The pleasure-principle is a tendency which subserves a certain function—namely, that of rendering the psychic apparatus as a whole free from any excitation, or to keep the amount of excitation constant or as low as possible.   *BPP—ch. 7*

The pleasure-pain principle is brought into action in response to the danger-signal, and plays a part in repression. . . . This principle has unrestricted sway over the processes in the id.   *NILP—ch. 4*

POISONING, FEAR OF—See *Weaning.*

PRECONSCIOUS—Everything unconscious that can easily exchange the unconscious condition for the conscious one, is better described as "capable of entering consciousness," or as *preconscious.*   *OoPA—ch. 4*

From a purely descriptive point of view, the "preconscious" is also unconscious, but we do not give it that name, except when we are speaking loosely, or when we have to defend in general the existence of unconscious processes in mental life.
                                    NILP—ch. 3

That which is latent, and only unconscious in the descriptive and not in the dynamic sense, we call *preconscious;* the term unconscious we reserve for the dynamically unconscious repressed, so that we now have three terms, conscious (Cs), preconscious (Pcs), and unconscious (Ucs), which are no longer purely descriptive in sense. *E & I—ch. 1*

See also *Ego and Its Relationship to the Preconscious.*

PRE-GENITAL PHASES—We will call the organizations of the sexual life in which the genital zones have not yet assumed the dominating role, the *pregenital phase.*

One of the first of such pregenital sexual organizations is the *oral,* or if one will, the cannabalistic. Here the sexual activity is not yet separated from the taking of nourishment and the contrasts within it are not yet differentiated. The object of the one activity is also that of the other; the sexual aim then consists in the *incorporation* of the object into one's own body, the prototype of *identification,* which later plays such an important psychic rôle. As a remnant of this fictitious phase of organization forced on us by pathology, we can consider thumbsucking. Here the sexual activity became separated from the nourishment activity and the strange object was given up in favor of one from his own body.

A second pregenital phase is the *sadistic-anal* organization. Here the contrasts which run through the whole sexual life are already developed, but cannot yet be designated as *masculine* and *feminine,* but must be called *active* and *passive.*

TCTS II

Third comes the *phallic* phase, in which for both sexes the penis (and what corresponds to it in the girl) achieves an importance which can no longer be overlooked. We have reserved the name of *genital* phase for the final sexual organization, established after puberty, in which the female genitals receive for the first time the recognition which the male genitals have long since obtained. *NILP—ch. 4*

PROCESSES, PRIMARY AND SECONDARY—Processes in the unconscious or in the id obey different laws from those in the preconscious ego. We name these laws in their totality the *primary process,* in contrast to the *secondary process* which regulates events in the preconscious or ego. *OoPA—ch. 4*

PROJECTION—See *Paranoia, Projection in.*

PSYCHIATRY—Psychiatry, alone, is concerned with the disturbances of mental functioning; but one knows in what way and with what purposes. Psychiatry looks for the physical causes of mental disorders and treats them like those of any other illness. *QLA—ch. 6*

PSYCHIC APPARATUS AND ITS FUNCTION—As the architectural principle of the psychic apparatus, we may conjecture a certain stratification or structure of instances deposited in strata. *PEL—ch. 7*

Certain inadequacies of our psychic functions and certain performances which are apparently unintentional prove to be well motivated when subjected to psychoanalytic investigation, and are determined through the consciousness of unknown motives.

In order to belong to the class of phenomena which can thus be explained, a faulty psychic action must satisfy the following conditions:

(a) It must not exceed a certain measure, which is firmly established through our estimation, and is designated by the expression "within normal limits."

(b) It must evince the character of the momentary and temporary disturbance. The same action must have been previously performed more correctly or we must always rely on ourselves to perform it more correctly; if we are corrected by others, we must immediately recognize the truth of the correction and the incorrectness of our psychic action.

(c) If we at all perceive a faulty action, we must not perceive in ourselves any motivation of the same, but must attempt to explain it through "inattention" or attribute it to an "accident."

Thus, there remain in this group the cases of forgetting, the errors, the lapses in speaking, reading, writing, the erroneously carried-out actions and the so-called chance actions. *PEL—ch. 12*

PSYCHIC MOTIVE POWER—The transformation of psychic motive power into the different forms of activity is perhaps as little convertible without loss, as in the case of physical forces. *LDV—ch. 1*

PSYCHOANALYSIS [cf. also ANALYSIS]—Psychoanalysis is the name (1) of a procedure for the investigation of mental processes which are almost inaccessible in any other way, (2) of a method (based upon that investigation) for the treatment of neurotic disorders and (3) of a collection of psy-

chological information obtained along those lines, which is gradually being accumulated into a new scientific discipline.
                                                                    PA

Psychoanalysis is a dynamic conception, which reduces mental life to the interplay of reciprocally urging and checking forces.   *PVD*

The contribution of psychoanalysis to science consists precisely in having extended research to the region of the mind.
                                                            NILP—ch. 7

Psychoanalysis is not, in my opinion, in a position to create a *Weltanschauung* of its own. It has no need to do so, for it is a branch of science, and can subscribe to the scientific *Weltanschauung*.   *NILP—ch. 7*

Psychoanalysis, Field of Application of—The field in which analytical therapy can be applied is that of the transference-neuroses, phobias, hysterias, obsessional neuroses, and besides these such abnormalities of character as have been developed instead of these diseases. Everything other than these, such as narcissistic or psychotic conditions, is more or less unsuitable.   *NILP—ch. 6*

The sphere of application of psychoanalysis extends as far as that of psychology, to which it forms a complement of the greatest moment.   *ABS—ch. 6*

The impulses and their transformations are the last things psychoanalysis can discern. Henceforth it leaves the stage to biological investigation.   *LVD—ch. 6*

Psychoanalysis, Objects and Aims of—The analysis aims at laying bare the complexes which have been repressed as a result of the painful feelings associated with them, and which produce signs of resistance when there is an attempt to bring them into consciousness.   *PA & CL*

It is one of the tasks of psychoanalysis to lift the veil of amnesia which shrouds the earliest years of childhood and to bring the expressions of infantile sexual life which are hidden behind it into conscious memory.   *NILP—ch. 1*

Psychoanalysis, Theory of—The whole of psychoanalytic theory is in fact built up on the perception of the resistance exerted by the patient when we try to make him conscious of his unconscious.   *NILP—ch. 3*

Psychoanalysis as a Therapeutic Method—One of the first applications of psychoanalysis was that we were able to understand the opposition we had to meet on account of our psychoanalytic activities. . . . Psychoanalysis originated as a therapeutic procedure; it has gone for beyond that, but it has never given up its original field of work, and it still relies upon contact with clinical material for its further advances and development. The accumulation of empirical data upon which we base our theories can be obtained in no other way. . . . Psychoanalysis really is a form of therapy, just as other methods are. . . . As a psychotherapeutic method, analysis does not stand in opposition to other methods employed in this branch of medicine; it does not invalidate them nor does it exclude them. . . . The practice of psychoanalysis is difficult and exacting! . . . As a rule psychoanalysis either possesses the doctor entirely or not at all. . . . Compared with other psychotherapeutic procedures, phychoanalysis is far and away the most powerful. In suitable cases one can remove disturbances, and bring about alterations which could not be hoped for in preanalytic times. But it has also perfectly clearly felt limitations.   *NILP—ch. 6*

No injury to the patient is to be feared when the treatment is conducted with real comprehension.   *PT*

PSYCHOLOGY

Psychology and Dreams—The psychology of the schools has never been able to say what dreams mean. It has not known what to do with them; if it tried to explain them, it had to become unpsychological, to fall back on sense-stimuli, unequal depth of sleep in the various parts of the brain, etc. But one may say that a psychology which cannot explain dreams is also useless for the elucidation of normal psychical activity, and has no claim to be called a science.   *QLA—ch. 2*

Psychology and the Id—Psychology blocked its own access to the sphere of the Id by holding to an assumption which seems natural, but is in fact untenable; namely, that all psychical acts are conscious, that what is mental is actually distinguished as such by the very fact of being conscious, and that, if unconscious processes do take place in our brains, these do not merit the name of mental acts.   *QLA—ch. 2*

PSYCHONEUROTIC SYMPTOMS [cf. NEUROSIS; NEUROTICS; SYMPTOMS]

Psychoneurotic Symptoms, Formation of—The theory of the psychoneuroses asserts with absolute certainty that it can only be sexual wish-impulses from the infantile life, which have undergone repression (affect-conversion) during the developmental period of childhood, which are capable of renewal at later periods of development (whether as a result of our sexual constitution, which has, of course, grown out of an original bi-sexuality, or in consequence of unfavorable influences in our sexual life); and which therefore supply the motive-power for all psychoneurotic symptom-formation.   *IOD—ch. 7*

Psychoneurotic Symptoms as Wish-Fulfillments—The theory of all psychoneurotic symptoms culminates in the one proposition *that they, too, must be conceived as wish-fulfillments of the unconscious.* (Expressed more exactly: One portion of the symptom corresponds to the unconscious wish-fulfillment, while the other corresponds to the reaction-formation opposed to it.)   *IoD—ch. 7*

PSYCHOSIS—In psychoses, the turning away from reality is brought about in two ways; either because the repressed unconscious is too strong, so that it overwhelms the conscious which tries to cling on to reality, or because reality has become so unbearably painful that the threatened ego, in a despairing gesture of opposition, throws itself into the arms of the unconscious impulses. [Cf. also *Neurosis and Psychosis.*]

NILP—ch. 1

PUNISHMENT, UNCONSCIOUS NEED FOR—As to the origin of the unconscious need for punishment, there can be, I think, no doubt. It behaves like a part of the conscience, like the prolongation of conscience into the unconscious; and it must have the same origin as conscience, that is to say it will correspond to a piece of aggressiveness which has been internalized and taken over by the super-ego. If only the words were less incongruous, we should be justified, for all practical purposes, in calling it "an unconscious sense of guilt." . . . People in whom this unconscious sense of guilt is d o m i n a n t, distinguish themselves under analytic treatment by exhibiting what is so unwelcome from the point of view of prognosis—a negative therapeutic reaction. [Cf. also *Guilt, Sense of.*]

NILP—ch. 4

The need for punishment is an instinctual manifestation on the part of the ego, which has become masochistic under the influence of the sadistic super-ego, i.e. which has brought a part of the instinct of destruction at work within itself into the service of an erotic attachment to the super-ego.

C & D—ch. 8

PUBERTY—The complete organization [of sexuality] is not attained until puberty, in a fourth, or genital, phase. A state of affairs is then established in which (1) many earlier libidinal cathexes are retained, (2) others are included in the sexual function as preparatory or auxiliary acts, their satisfaction producing what is known as fore-pleasure, and (3) other tendencies are excluded from the organization, and are either entirely suppressed (repressed) or are employed in the ego in some other way, forming character-traits or undergoing sublimation with a displacement of their aims.   *OoPA—ch. 3*

Puberty forms a definite epoch in the development of the compulsion neurosis. The genital organization, interrupted in childhood, is now resumed with great vigor.   *PoA—ch. 5*

Q

QUACK—In the eyes of the law, a quack is one who treats patients without being able to produce a State medical degree. I should prefer another definition: a quack is a person who undertakes a treatment without possessing the knowledge and capacity required for it.

QLA—ch. 6

R

RACE AND THE INDIVIDUAL—Important biological analogies have taught us that the psychic development of the individual is a short repetition of the course of development of the race.   *LDV—ch. 3*

RACIAL MEMORY—There probably exists in the mental life of the individual not only what he has experienced himself, but also what he brought with him at birth, fragments of phylogenetic origin, an archaic heritage. . . . The archaic heritage of mankind includes not only dispositions, but also ideational contents, memory traces of the experiences of former generations.   *M & M—Part III, Section I*

REALITY PRINCIPLE—In taming the impulses of the Id, the Ego replaces the pleasure principle, which was earlier the sole regulating factor, by the so-called *reality principle,* which indeed pursues the same ends but takes into account the conditions imposed by the outer world.   *QLA—ch. 3*

REFLECTION—I have noticed in the course of my psychoanalytical work that the psychological state of a man in an attitude of reflection is entirely different from that of a man who is observing his psychic processes. In reflection there is a greater play of psychic activity than in the most attentive self-observation; this is shown even by the tense attitude and the wrinkled brow of the man in a state of reflection, as opposed to the mimic tranquillity of the man observing himself.

IoD—ch. 2

REGRESSION—As to the regression, we may further observe that it plays a no less important part in the theory of neurotic symptom-formation than in the theory of dreams. We may therefore distinguish a threefold species of regression: (*a*) a *topical* one, in the sense of the scheme of the ψ-systems here

expounded; (b) a *temporal* one, in so far as it is a regression
to older psychic formations; and (c) a *formal* one, when
primitive modes of expression and representation take the
place of the customary modes. These three forms of regression
are, however, basically one, and in the majority of cases they
coincide, for that which is older in point of time is at the same
time formally primitive and, in the psychic topography, nearer
to the perception-end.   *IoD—ch. 7*

Regression to Childhood; Regression to the Uterus—See
Agoraphobia.

Regression in Dreams—In regression the structure of the
dream-thoughts breaks up into its raw material.
                                                IoD—ch. 7

Regression of Instinctual Impulses—In compulsion neurosis there is brought about, under the influence of the ego's
opposition, a regression of the instinctual impulses to an earlier
libidinal phase such as does not, it is true, make repression
superfluous, but evidently operates to the same effect as
repression.   *PoA—ch. 11*

Regression, Temporal—When we investigate psychoneurotic conditions, we find in each of them occasion to comment
upon a so-called *temporal regression, i.e.* the particular extent
to which each of them retraces the stages of its evolution. We
distinguish two such regressions—one in the development of
the ego and the other in that of the libido. In sleep, the latter
is carried to the point of restoring the primitive narcissism,
while the former goes back to the state of hallucinatory wish-
fulfilment.   *MSTD*

RELIGION—The derivation of a need for religion from the
child's feeling of helplessness and the longing it evokes for a
father seems to me incontrovertible, especially since this feeling is not simply carried on from childhood days but is kept
alive perpetually by the fear of what the superior power of
fate will bring.   *C & D—ch. 1*

Religion is an attempt to get control over the sensory world,
in which we are placed, by means of the wish-world which we
have developed inside us as a result of biological and psychological necessities. But it cannot achieve its end. Its doctrines

carry with them the stamp of the times in which they originated the ignorant childhood days of the human race. Its consolations deserve no trust. . . . If one attempts to assign to religion its place in man's evolution, it seems not so much to be a lasting acquisition, as a parallel to the neurosis which the civilized individual must pass through on his way from childhood to maturity.   *NILP—ch. 7*

See also *Totemisms as the Earliest Religion.*

Religion and Neurosis—Religious phenomena are to be understood only on the model of the neurotic symptoms of the individual, which are so familiar to us, as a return of long-forgotten important happenings in the primeval history of the human family, that they owe their obsessive character to that very origin and therefore derive their effect on mankind from the historical truth they contain.
M & M—Part III, Section II

One might venture to regard the obsessional neurosis as a pathological counterpart to the formation of a religion, to describe this neurosis as a private religious system, and religion as a universal obsessional neurosis.   *OA & RL*

It is easy to see wherein lies the resemblance between neurotic ceremonial and religious rites; it is in the fear of pangs of conscience after their omission, in the complete isolation of them from all other activities (the feeling that one must not be disturbed), and in the conscientiousness with which the details are carried out.   *OA & RL*

REMORSE—Remorse is a general term denoting the ego's reaction under a special form of the sense of guilt; it includes the almost unaltered sensory material belonging to the anxiety that is at work behind the sense of guilt; it is itself a punishment; it too, therefore, may occur before conscience has developed.   *C & D—ch. 8*

RENUNCIATION, INSTINCTUAL—When the Id makes an instinctual demand of an erotic or aggressive nature on a human being, the most simple and natural response for the Ego, which governs the apparatus for thinking and muscle innervation, is to satisfy this by an action. This satisfaction of the instinct is felt as pleasure by the Ego, just as not satisfying this instinct would undoubtedly become a source of discomfort.

Now, it may happen that the Ego eschews satisfaction of the instinct because of external obstacles—namely, when it realizes that the action in question would bring in its course serious danger to the Ego. Such a refraining from satisfaction, an "instinctual renunciation" because of external obstacles—as we say, in obedience to the reality-principle—is never pleasurable. The instinctual renunciation would bring about a lasting painful tension if we did not succeed in diminishing the strength of the instinctual urge itself through a displacement of energy. This instinctual renunciation may also be forced on us, however, by other motives, which we rightly call inner ones. In the course of individual development a part of the inhibiting forces in the outer world becomes internalized; a standard is created in the Ego which opposes the other faculties by observation, criticism, and prohibition. We call this new standard the *Super-ego*. . . . While, however, instinctual renunciation for external reasons is only painful, renunciation for internal reasons, in obedience to the demands of the Super-ego, has another economic effect. It brings besides the inevitable pain a gain in pleasure to the Ego—as it were, a substitutive satisfaction.

M & M—Part III, Section II

Instinctual Renunciation and Religion—*See Totemism as the Earliest Religion.*

REPETITION-COMPULSION—Endeavors to make the psychic trauma real—to live through once more a repetition of it; if it was an early affective relationship it is revived in an analogous connection with another person.

M & M—Part III, Section I

We are able to postulate the principle of a *repetition-compulsion* in the unconscious mind, based upon instinctual activity and probably inherent in the very nature of the instincts—a principle powerful enough to overrule the pleasure-principle, lending to certain aspects of the mind their daemonic character, and still very clearly expressed in the tendencies of small children; a principle, too, which is responsible for a part of the course taken by the analyses of neurotic patients.

Uncanny

We may assume that as soon as a given state of things is upset there arises an instinct to recreate it, and phenomena appear which we may call "repetition-compulsion."

NILP—ch. 4

REPRESSED—To the repressed we must rather ascribe a strong upward-driving force, an impulsion to get through to consciousness.   *NILP—ch. 3*

The repressed is only cut off sharply from the ego by the resistances of repression; it can communicate with the ego through the id.   *E & I—ch. 2*

See also *Id and Its Relation to the Unconscious; Repression.*

Repressed, Emergence into Consciousness of the—The repressed material retains its impetus to penetrate into consciousness. It reaches its aim when three conditions are present: (1) When the strength of counter-cathexis is diminished by an illness which acts on the Ego itself, or through a different distribution of cathexis in the Ego, as happens regularly during sleep. (2) When those instincts attached to the repressed material become strengthened. The processes during puberty provide the best example for this. (3) Whenever recent events produce impressions or experiences which are so much like the repressed material that they have the power to awaken it. Thus the recent material gets strengthened by the latent energy of the repressed and the repressed material produces its effect behind the recent material and with its help.   *M & M—Part III, Section I*

Repressed, Return of the—All phenomena of [neurotic] symptom-formation can be fairly described as "the return of the repressed."   *M & M—Part III, Section II*

REPRESSION—The infantile ego, under the domination of the external world, disposes of undesirable instinctual demands by means of what are called repressions.   *OoPA—ch. 8*

The essence of repression lies simply in the function of rejecting and keeping something out of consciousness.   *Repr*

The theory of repression became the foundation-stone of our understanding of the neuroses. . . . It is possible to take repression as a centre and to bring all the elements of psychoanalytical theory into relation with it.   *ABS—ch. 3*

Repression takes place in two distinct situations, namely, when an unwelcome instinctual impulse is aroused by an external perception, and when the impulse arises internally without such provocation.   *PoA—ch. 2*

Decisive repressions all occur in early childhood.

QLA—ch. 3

Repression . . . is, at bottom, an attempt at flight.

PoA—ch. 10

The Ego feels a demand from an instinct which it wishes to withstand, because it suspects that satisfaction is dangerous, would evoke a traumatic situation, a collision with the outer world; but it cannot master it, because it has not yet the strength necessary. The Ego then treats the risk from the instinct as though it were an outside danger, and makes an attempt at flight; it withdraws from that part of the Id, leaving it to its fate, after having refused it all the help which it normally affords to instinctual impulses. We put it, that Ego undertakes a *repression* of these instinctual impulses. By the act of repression the Ego follows the pleasure principle, which otherwise it is wont to correct, and it suffers harm on this account. The harm consists in the fact that the Ego has now imposed a lasting limitation on its sphere of power. The repressed instinctual impulse is henceforth isolated; it is left to itself and inaccessible, but this means that it cannot be influenced. It goes its own way.

QLA—ch. 3

Repression proceeds from the ego, which, possibly at the command of the superego, does not wish to be a party to an instinct cathexis originating in the id. Through repression the ego accomplishes the exclusion from consciousness of the idea which was the carrier of the unwelcome impulse. Analysis frequently demonstrates that the idea has been retained as an unconscious formation.

PoA—ch. 2

It is an important element of the theory of repression that this process is not one which takes place on a single occasion but is one demanding a continuous expenditure of effort.

PoA—ch. 10

See also *Repressed; Anxiety and Repression.*

Repression with Amnesia—See *Isolation.*

Repression, Ego and—As I understand it, in repression the ego functions under the influence of external reality and therefore excludes the result of the substitutive process from this reality.

The ego controls the entrance into consciousness as well as

the passage into activity directed to the environment; in repression it exerts its power at both places. The instinct representative experiences the one, the instinctual impulse itself the other side of the ego's manifestation of authority.

PoA—ch. 2

Repression, Ego and Id and—In the case of repression the fact of crucial importance is that the ego is an organized entity, whereas the id is not; in fact, the ego is the organized part of the id. It would be quite unjustifiable to conceive of the ego and the id as if they were two opposing camps—as though through repression the ego were seeking to suppress a part of the id, and that thereupon the rest of the id came to the assistance of the part attacked and measured its strength against that of the ego.

PoA—ch. 3

Repression, Primal—The majority of repressions with which we have to do in therapeutic work are instances of *subsequential* repression. They presuppose *primal* repressions of an earlier date which exercise over the more recent situation their gravitative influence.

PoA—ch. 2

Repression, Subsequential—See *Repression, Primal.*

Repression, Superego and—Now we have posited a special function within the ego to represent the demand for restriction and rejection, *i.e.* the super-ego, we can say that repression is the work of the super-ego,—either that it does its work on its own account or else that the ego does it in obedience to its orders.

NILP—ch. 3

Repression, Tendency to—The tendency to repression . . . must be traced back to the organic bases of the character, upon which alone the psychic structure rises.

LDV—ch. 6

REPRESSION-RESISTANCE — Ego's repression-resistance (that is, the unpleasure felt by it at undertaking the severe work imposed upon it).

OoPA—ch. 6

The ego protects itself against the incursion of undesirable elements from the unconscious and repressed id by means of anti-cathexes, which must remain intact if it is to function normally. The more hardly the ego feels itself pressed, the more convulsively it clings (in terror, as it were) to these anti-cathexes, in order to protect what remains of it from further irruptions. . . . The ego shrinks from undertakings that seem dangerous and threaten unpleasure; it must be constantly spurred on and soothed down if it is not to fail us. This resistance, which persists through the whole treatment and is renewed with every fresh piece of work, has been named, though not quite correctly, *repression-resistance.* *OoPA—ch. 6*

RESISTANCE IN ANALYSIS—The whole of psychoanalytic theory is in fact built up on the perception of the resistance exerted by the patient when we try to make him conscious of his unconscious. The objective indication of resistance is that his associations stop short or wander far away from the theme that is being discussed. He may also become subjectively aware of the resistance by experiencing painful feelings when he approaches the theme. But this last indication may be absent.
NILP—ch. 3

We call all the forces which oppose the work of cure the patient's "resistances." The gain from the illness is the source of one resistance, and "unconscious guilt" represents the resistance from the Super-Ego; this is the most powerful factor, and the one we most fear. We meet still other resistances in the course of the treatment. If the Ego, in the early period, undertook a repression on account of anxiety, that anxiety still exists, and now expresses itself as a resistance if the Ego approaches what is repressed. It may well be imagined that difficulties arise when an instinctual process, which has followed a certain path perhaps for decades, is suddenly required to take a new course which has now opened for it. One might call that the resistance of the Id. The fight against all these resistances is the main work in the treatment, and the task of interpretation seems small beside it. *QLA—ch. 4*

The overcoming of resistance is the part of our work which requires the greatest time and the greatest trouble.
OoPA—ch. 6

The fifth type of resistance . . . of the superego, the last recognized and the most obscure, but not always the weakest, seems to derive from the sense of guilt or need of punishment; it resists any success and hence also recovery through the analysis. *PoA—ch. 11*

[See also *Ego-Resistance, Repression-Resistance.*]

RESISTANCE IN DREAM-INTERPRETATION—A resistance is the sure sign of a conflict. There must be a force present which is trying to express something, and another which is striving to prevent its expression.   *NILP—ch. 1*

RESISTANCE OF THE UNCONSCIOUS—After the cessation of the ego-resistance there is still the power of the repetition compulsion, the attraction exerted by its unconscious prototypes upon the repressed instinctual process, to be overcome; nor is it in any way inconsistent with this to designate this factor as the *resistance of the unconscious.*   *PoA—ch. 11*

RESPONSIBILITY, JURIDICAL—See *Social Institutions.*

RETURN OF THE REPRESSED—See *Repressed, Return of.*

S

SADISM—The roots of active algolagnia, sadism, can be readily demonstrable in the normal individual. The sexuality of most men shows an admixture of aggression, of a desire to subdue, the biological significance of which lies in the necessity for overcoming the resistance of the sexual object by actions other than mere *courting*. Sadism would then correspond to an aggressive component of the sexual instinct which has become independent and exaggerated and has been brought to the foreground by displacement.

The concept of sadism fluctuates in everyday speech from a mere active or impetuous attitude towards the sexual object to an absolute attachment of the gratification to the subjection and maltreatment of the object. Stricly speaking, only the last extreme case can claim the name of perversion.   *TCTS I*

SADISTIC-ANAL PHASE—See *Pregenital Phases.*

SCIENCE—Scientific thought is, in its essence, no different from the normal process of thinking, which we all, believers and unbelievers, alike, make use of when we are going about our business in everyday life. . . . Its aim is to arrive at correspondence with reality, that is to say with what exists outside us and independently of us, and as experience has taught us, is decisive for the fulfilment or frustration of our desires. This correspondence with the real external world we call truth.
NILP—ch. 7

SCREEN-MEMORY- -The period of infantile amnesia is often interrupted by isolated fragmentary memories, the so-called "screen-memories."   *M & M—Part III, Section I*

"SELF-ANALYSIS"—We consider that everyone who wishes to treat others by analysis should first undergo an analysis himself. Only in the course of this "self-analysis" (as it is mistakently termed), when he actually experiences in his own person, or rather in his own psyche, the processes asserted by analysis to take place, does he acquire the convictions by which he will be later guided as an analyst.   *QLA—ch. 2*

SELF-REFERENCE COMPLEX—See *Forgetting of Names.*

SENSATION—Cf. *Perception.*

SENSE-PERCEPTION—Cf. *Perception.*

SEX AND SOCIETY—I know, of course, that the recognition we afford to sexuality is—whether they confess it or not—the strongest motive for our opponents' hostility to psychoanalysis. But are we to let ourserves be shaken on that account? It only shows us how neurotic our whole cultural life is, when people apparently normal behave no differently from neurotics.
QLA—ch. 4

SEX ACT—The union of the genitals in the characteristic act of copulation is taken as the normal sexual aim. It serves to diminish the sexual tension and to quench temporarily the sexual desire (gratification analogous to satisfaction of hunger). Yet, even in the most normal sexual act, certain addenda are distinguishable, the development of which may lead to aberrations described as *perversions.*   *TCTS I*

The execution of the sex act presupposes a very complicated sequence of events, any one of which may be the locus of disturbance.   *PoA—ch. 1*

SEXUAL AIM—The aim towards which the [sexual] instinct strives.   *TCTS I*

Sexual Aim, Infantile—Consists in the production of gratification through the proper excitation of this or that selected erogenous zone.   *TCTS II*

SEXUAL EXCITEMENT—Sexual excitement is the expression of libidinal instinctual impulses.
PoA—ch. 4

SEXUAL FUNCTION, IMPAIRMENT OF—The most varied means are employed to impair function, as: (1) the mere turning aside of libido, which seems most easily to produce what we call pure inhibition; (2) impairment of the execution of the function; (3) the rendering it difficult through the imposition of special conditions, and its modification through diverting it to other aims; (4) its prevention by means of precautionary measures; (5) its discontinuance by the development of anxiety, when the initiation of the function can no longer be prevented; finally, (6) a subsequent reaction of protest against the act and a desire to undo it if it has actually been carried out. *PoA—ch. 1*

SEXUAL IMPULSES—Observation of daily life shows us that most persons have the capacity to direct a very tangible part of their sexual motive powers to their professional or business activities. The sexual impulse is particularly suited to yield such contributions because it is endowed with the capacity of sublimation, i.e., it has the power to exchange its nearest aim for others of higher value which are not sexual. We consider this process as proved, if the history of childhood or the history of the psychic development of a person shows that in his childhood this powerful impulse was in the service of sexual interest. We consider it a further corroboration if the sexual life of mature years evinces a striking stunting, as if a part of the sexual activity had now been replaced by the activity of the predominant impulse. *LDV—ch. 1*

Most of the impulses of sexual life are not of a purely erotic nature but arise from alloys of the erotic instinct with components of the destructive instinct. *OoPA—ch. 7*

SEXUAL INSTINCT AND LIBIDO—The fact of sexual need in man and animal is expressed in biology by the assumption of a "sexual instinct." This instinct is made analogous to the instinct of taking nourishment, and to hunger. The sexual expression corresponding to hunger not being found colloquially, science uses the expression, "libido." *TCTS I*

SEXUAL LIFE—The sexual life of the human being does not develop in progressive fashion from incipience to maturity, as in the case of most of the closely related animals, but it suffers an abrupt interruption after an initial early florescence extending to about the fifth year, after which it commences anew with puberty, dovetailing, as it were, with the tendencies of the infantile period. *PoA—ch. 10*

Sexual Life and Civilization—The sexual life of civilized man is seriously disabled, whatever we may say; it sometimes makes an impression of being a function in process of becoming atrophied, just as organs like our teeth and our hair seem to be. *C & D—ch. 4*

Sexual Life, Double Onset of—See *Sexuality in Childhood*.

Sexual Life and Phobia—Phobias do not occur at all when the *vita sexualis* is normal.   *RCA-N*

SEXUAL OBJECT—The person from whom the sexual attraction emanates.   *TCTS I*

Sexual Object, Unfit Substitutes for—We are especially impressed by those cases in which the normal sexual object is substituted for another, which, though related to it, is totally unfit for the normal sexual aim.

The substitute for the sexual object is generally a part of the body but little adapted for sexual purposes, such as the foot or hair or some inanimate object (fragments of clothing, underwear), which has some demonstrable relation to the sexual person, preferably to the sexuality of the same. This substitute is not unjustly compared with the fetich in which the savage sees the embodiment of his god.

The case becomes pathological only when the striving for the fetich fixes itself beyond such determinations and takes the place of the normal sexual aim; or again, when the fetich disengages itself from the person concerned and itself becomes a sexual object. These are the general determinants for the transition of mere variations of the sexual instinct to pathological aberrations.   *TCTS I*

[Cf. *Fetishism*.]

SEXUALITY—Among the causes of and occasions for neurotic complaints sexual factors play an important, an overweening—even perhaps a specific—rôle.   *QLA—ch. 4*

Sexual life does not begin only at puberty, but starts with clear manifestations soon after birth.

It is necessary to distinguish sharply between the concepts of "sexual" and "genital." The former is the wider concept and includes many activities that have nothing to do with the genitals.

Sexual life comprises the function of obtaining pleasure from zones of the body—a function which is subsequently brought into the service of that of reproduction. The two functions often fail to coincide completely.   *OoPA—ch. 3*

Sexuality, Female—There can be no doubt that the bisexual disposition which we maintain to be characteristic of human beings manifests itself much more plainly in the female than in the male. The latter has only one principal sexual zone —only one sexual organ—whereas the former has two: the vagina, the true female organ, and the clitoris, which is analogous to the male organ. We believe that we may justly assume that for many years the vagina is virtually non-existent and possibly remains without sensation until puberty.   *FS*

Sexuality in Childhood—The sexual instinctual impulses accompany life from birth, and it is just these instincts against which the infantile Ego undertakes defense by repressions.
QLA—ch. 4

The child brings along into the world germs of sexual activity and even while taking nourishment, it at the same time also enjoys a sexual gratification which it then seeks again to procure for itself through the familiar activity of "thumb-sucking." The sexual activity of the child, however, does not develop in the same measure as his other functions, but merges first into the so-called latency period from the age of three to the age of five years. The production of sexual excitation by no means ceases at this period but continues to furnish a stock of energy, the greater part of which is utilized for aims other than sexual. On the one hand, it is used for the delivery of sexual components for social feelings, and on the other hand (by means of repression and reaction formation), for the erection of the future sex barriers. Accordingly, the forces which are destined to hold the sexual instinct in certain tracks are built up in fancy with the help of education at the expense of the greater part of the perverse sexual feelings. Another part of the infantile sexual manifestations escapes this utilization and may manifest itself as sexual activity. It can then be discovered that the sexual excitation of the child flows from diverse sources. Above all, gratifications originate through the adapted sensible excitation of so-called erogenous zones. For these probably any skin region or sensory organ may serve; but there are certain distinguished erogenous zones, the excitation of which by certain organic mechanisms, is assured from the beginning. Moreover, sexual excitation originates in the organism, as it were, as a by-product in a greater number of processes, as soon as they attain a certain intensity; this especially takes place in all strong emotional excitements, even if they be of a painful nature. The excitations from all these sources do not yet unite, but they pursue their aim individually

—this aim consisting merely in the gaining of a certain pleasure. The sexual instinct of childhood is therefore objectless or *autoerotic*.   *TCTS III*

A child's sexual life is naturally different from that of an adult. The sexual function undergoes a complicated development between its beginnings and the final form which we recognize as familiar. It grows together out of a number of component instincts with special aims, and passes through several phases of organization, until finally it is brought into the service of reproduction. The individual component-instincts are not all equally useful for the final purpose, and they must be diverted, remodelled, and in part suppressed. Such a far-reaching development is not always faultlessly carried out, and there may be inhibitions of development and partial fixations at early stages; where, later, the exercise of the sexual function is met by hindrances, the sexual striving—the libido, as we say—reverts to such earlier points of fixation. The study of childhood sexuality, and its changes on the way to maturity, has also given us the key to the understanding of the so-called sexual perversions.   *QLA—ch. 4*

The most remarkable feature—as it seems to me—in children's sexual life is that it runs its whole far-reaching course in the first five years of life. From then on, until puberty, it goes through the so-called latency period, in which, normally, sexuality makes no progress; on the contrary, the sexual strivings diminish in strength, and much that the child practiced or knew before is given up and forgotten. In this period, after the early blooming of sexual life has withered, are built up such attitudes of the Ego as shame, disgust, and morality, destined to stand against the later storms of puberty and to direct the paths of the freshly-awakened sexual desires. This so-called *double onset of sexual life* has much to do with the rise of neurotic ailments.   *QLA—ch. 4*

A further characteristic of the sexuality of early childhood is that the female organ as yet plays no part in it—the child has not yet discovered it. All the accent falls on the male organ, and all interest is concentrated on whether it is present or not.
                                                           QLA—ch. 4

A child's sexual impulses find their main outlet in gratification on its own body, by stimulation of its own genitals—in actual fact, the male component of the genitals.   *QLA—ch. 4*

. . . . psychoanalytic investigation . . . teaches us that many, perhaps most, children, at least the most gifted ones, go through a period beginning with the third year, which may be designated as the period of *infantile sexual investigation*. As far as we know, this curiosity is not awakened spontaneously in children of this age. It is aroused through the impression of an important experience, through the birth of a little brother or sister, or through fear of the same engendered by some outward experience, wherein the child sees a danger to his egotistic interests. The investigation directs itself to the question whence children come, as if the child were looking for means to guard against such an undesired event. . . . If the period of infantile sexual investigation comes to an end through an impetus of energetic sexual repression, the early association with sexual interest may result in three different possibilities for the future fate of the investigation impulse. The investigation either shares the fate of the sexuality; the curiosity henceforth remains inhibited and the free activity of intelligence may become narrowed for life. This is especially favored shortly thereafter by education and powerful religious inhibitions. This is the type of neurotic inhibition. . . . In a second type the intellectual development is sufficiently strong to withstand the sexual repression pulling at it. Sometimes, after the disappearance of the infantile sexual investigation, it offers its support to the old association in order to elude sexual repression, and the suppressed sexual investigation comes back from the unconscious as compulsive reasoning. It is naturally distorted and not free, but forceful enough to sexualize even thought itself and to accentuate the intellectual operations with the pleasure and anxiety of the actual sexual processes. Here the investigation becomes sexual activity and often exclusively so; the feeling of settling the problem and of explaining things in the mind is put in place of sexual gratification. But the indeterminate character of the infantile investigation repeats itself also in the fact that this reasoning never ends, and that the desired intellectual feeling of the solution constantly recedes into the distance.

By virtue of a special disposition the third, which is the most rare and most perfect type, escapes the inhibition of thought and the compulsive reasoning. Also here sexual repression takes place, but it does not succeed in evincing a partial impulse of the sexual pleasure in the unconscious; instead the libido withdraws from the fate of the repression by being sublimated from the outset into curiosity, and by reinforcing the powerful investigation impulse.   *LDV—ch. 1*

What attitude ought we to take towards the sexual indulgence of early childhood? We have become aware of the responsibility we incur by suppressing it, and yet we cannot assume that it is right to allow it unchecked. It appears that among races of low culture, and in the lower strata of civilized peoples, children's sexuality is allowed free play. That probably constitutes a strong protection against later lapses into individual neurosis, but is there not at the same time great detriment to the aptitude for cultural achievement? There is a good deal which goes to suggest that in this respect we are between a new Scylla and Charybdis.   *QLA—ch. 4*

Second Phase of Childhood Masturbation. Infantile masturbation seems to disappear after a brief time, but it may continue uninterruptedly till puberty and thus represent the first marked deviation from that development which is desirable for civilized man. At some time during childhood after the nursing period, the sexual instinct of the genitals reawakens and continues active for some time until it is again suppressed, or it may continue without interruption.
                                                           TCTS II

Sexuality, Infantile—See *Sexuality in Childhood.*

Sexuality in Puberty—With the beginning of puberty, changes set in, which transform the infantile sexual life into its definite normal form. Hitherto, the sexual instinct has been preponderantly autoerotic; it now finds the sexual object. Thus far, it has manifested itself in single impulses and in erogenous zones seeking a certain pleasure as a single sexual aim. A new sexual aim now appears for the production of which all partial impulses cooperate, while the erogenous zones subordinate themselves to the primacy of the genital zone. As the new sexual aim assigns very different functions to the two sexes, their sexual developments now part company. The male sexual development is more consistent and easier to understand, while in the woman a sort of regression seems to appear. The normality of the sexual life is guaranteed only by the exact concurrence of the two streams directed to the sexual object and sexual aim. It is like the piercing of a tunnel from opposite sides.

The new sexual aim in the man consists in the discharge of the sexual products. This is not contradictory to the former sexual aim, which is that of obtaining pleasure; on the contrary, the height of all pleasure is connected with this final act in the sexual process. The sexual instinct now enters into the service of the function of propagation; it becomes, so to say, altruistic. If this transformation is to succeed, its process must be adjusted to the original dispositions and all the peculiarities of the impulses. *TCTS III*

Let us finally add that during the transition period of puberty the somatic and psychic processes of development proceed side by side, but separately, until with the breaking through of an intense psychic love-stimulus for the innervation of the genitals, the normally demanded unification of the erotic function is established. *TCTS III*

SHAME—The age of childhood, in which the sense of shame is unknown, seems a paradise when we look back upon it later, and paradise itself is nothing but the mass-phantasy of the childhood of the individual. This is why in paradise men are naked and unashamed, until the moment arrives when shame and fear awaken; expulsion follows, and sexual life and cultural development begin. Into this paradise dreams can take us back every night; we have already ventured the conjecture that the impressions of our earliest childhood (from the prehistoric period until about the end of the third year) crave reproduction for their own sake, perhaps without further reference to their content, so that their repetition is a wish-fulfilment. Dreams of nakedness, then, are *exhibition-dreams*.
IoD—ch. 5

SLEEP—The necessary mental pre-condition of sleep is the concentration of the ego upon the wish to sleep and the withdrawal of psychical energy from all the interests of life; since at the same time all the paths of approach to motility are blocked, the ego is also able to reduce the expenditure of energy by which at other times it maintains the repressions.
ABS—ch. 4

The state of sleep makes dream-formation possible by reducing the endopsychic censorship. *IoD—ch. 7*

The thought-impulses continued into sleep may be divided into the following groups:
1. Those which have not been completed during the day, owing to some accidental cause.
2. Those which have been left uncompleted because our mental powers have failed us, i.e. unsolved problems.
3. Those which have been turned back and suppressed

during the day. This is reinforced by a powerful fourth group:

4. Those which have been excited in our *Ucs.* during the day by the workings of the *Pcs;* and finally we may add a fifth, consisting of:

5. The indifferent impressions of the day, which have therefore been left unsettled.   *IoD—ch. 7*

The state of sleep represents a turning away from the real external world, and thus provides a necessary condition for the development of a psychosis.   *NILP—ch. 1*

The fact of dream-censorship shows that enough repressive resistance remains operative even during sleep.
                    NILP—ch. 1

[See also *Dream and Sleep.*]

Sleep as Return to the Womb—We shall be justified in saying that there arises at birth an instinct to return to the intrauterine life that has been abandoned—an instinct to sleep. Sleep is a return of this kind to the womb.
                    OoPA--ch. 5

SLEEP-WISH—The wish to sleep, to which the conscious ego has adjusted itself, and which (together with the dream-censorship and the "secondary elaboration" to be mentioned later) represents the ego's contribution to the dream, must thus always be taken into account as a motive of dream-formation, and every successful dream is a fulfilment of this wish.
                    IoD—ch. 5

SLIP OF THE TONGUE—The lapse in speech . . . is without doubt a motor function.   *PEL—ch. 8*

We find that, in order to explain a slip of the tongue, for instance, we are obliged to assume that an intention to say some particular thing had formed itself in the mind of the person who made the slip. We can infer it with certainty from the occurrence of the speech-disturbance, but it was not able to obtain expression; it was, that is to say, unconscious.
                    NILP—ch. 3

What we observe in normal persons as slips of the tongue gives the same impression as the first step of the so-called "paraphasias" which manifest themselves under pathologic conditions.   *PEL—ch. 5*

The speech disturbance which manifests itself as a speech-blunder may, in the first place, be caused by the influence of another component of the same speech; that is, through a foresound or an echo, or through another meaning within the sentence or context which differs from that which the speaker wishes to utter. In the second place, however, the disturbance could be brought about through influences outside this word, sentence or context, from elements which we did not intend to express, and of whose incitement we became conscious only through the disturbance. In both modes of origin of the mistake in speech, the common element lies in the simultaneity of the stimulus, while the differentiating elements lie in the arrangement within or without the same sentence or context.

PEL—ch. 5

SOCIAL INSTITUTIONS—All our social institutions are cut to the pattern of people with a unified, normal Ego, which one can classify as good or bad, and which either fulfills its function or is disabled by an overpowering influence. Hence the juridical alternative—responsible or not responsible.

QLA—ch. 5

[Cf. *Sex and Society*.]

SOMATIC PROCESSES—[Psychoanalysis] explains the supposed somatic accessory processes as being what is essentially mental and disregards for the moment the quality of consciousness.

OoPA—ch. 4

SOMATIC STIMULI AND DREAM—See *Dream, Effect of External Stimuli on; Dream, Influence of Somatic Stimuli on.*

SPEECH—. . . . the function of speech . . . brings the material in the ego into a firm connection with the memory-traces of visual and more particularly of auditory perceptions.

OoPA—ch. 4

Speech in the Dream—When in a dream something has the character of a spoken utterance—that is, when it is said or heard, not merely thought—and the distinction can usually be made with certainty—then it originates in the utterances of waking life, which have, of course, been treated as raw material, dismembered, and slightly altered, and above all removed from their context.

IoD—ch. 5

SPEECH-BLUNDER—See also *Slip of the Tongue*.
There is no doubt that the disturbances of the speech func-

tions occur more easily and make less demand on the disturbing forces than other psychic acts.   *PEL—ch. 10*

SUBCONSCIOUS—When someone talks of the subconscious, I do not know whether he means it topographically, as what lies in the psyche below consciousness, or qualitatively, as another consciousness—a subterranean one as it were. Probably he is not clear on the point himself. The only admissible antithesis is between conscious and unconscious. But it would be a serious error to suppose that this distinction coincides with that between the Ego and the Id.   *QLA—ch. 2*

SUBLIMATION—Sublimation is a process that concerns the object-libido and consists in the instinct's directing itself towards an aim other than, and remote from, that of sexual gratification; in this process the accent falls upon the deflection from the sexual aim.   *Narc*

The process through which the excessive excitations from individual sexual sources are discharged and utilized in other spheres, so that no small enhancement of mental capacity results from a predisposition which is dangerous as such.
          TCTS III

The tendency to repression, as well as the ability to sublimate, must be traced back to the organic bases of the character, upon which alone the psychic structure arises.
          LDV—ch. 6

SUGGESTION (SUGGESTIBILITY)—Suggestion (or more correctly suggestibility) is actually an irreducible, primitive phenomenon, a fundamental fact in the mental life of man.
          GPAE—ch. 3

What distinguishes a suggestion from other kinds of mental influence, such as a command or the giving of a piece of information or instruction, is that in the case of a suggestion an idea is aroused in another person's brain which is not examined in regard to its origin but is accepted just as though it had arisen spontaneously in that brain.   *H & S*

SUICIDE—There are some neurotics in whom, to judge by all their reactions, the instinct of self-preservation has actually been reversed. They seem to have nothing in view but self-injury and self-destruction. It is possible that people who in the end do in fact commit suicide belong to this group.
          OoPA—ch. 1

SUPEREGO—In the course of the individual development a part of the inhibiting forces in the outer world becomes internalized; a standard is created in the Ego which opposes the other faculties by observation, criticism, and prohibition. We call this new standard the Super-ego.

M & M—Part III, Section II

The Superego is the successor and representative of the parents (and educators) who superintended the actions of the individual in his first years of life; it perpetuates their functions almost without a change.

M & M—Part III, Section II

When I set out the relationship of Ego and Id I kept back an important part of the theory of the psychical apparatus. It is this: we were forced to assume that in the Ego itself a special agency has become differentiated, which we name the Super-Ego. This Super-Ego holds a special position between the Ego and the Id. It belongs to the Ego, shares its high psychological organization, but stands in an especially intimate connection with the Id. It is, actually, the precipitate of the Ego's first attachments to objects; the heir of the Œdipus complex, when that has been vacated. This Super-Ego can set itself against the Ego. It can treat it as an object, and often uses it very harshly. It is just as important for the Ego to live in concord with the Super-Ego as with the Id. Discords between Ego and Super-Ego have great significance for psychical life. You will have guessed by now that the Super-Ego is the vehicle for the phenomenon we call "conscience." It is very important for mental health that the Super-Ego should develop normally —that is, that it should become sufficiently depersonalized. It is precisely this that does not happen in the case of a neurotic, because his Œdipus complex does not undergo the right transformation. His Super-Ego deals with his Ego like a strict father with a child, and his idea of morality displays itself in primitive ways by making the Ego submit to punishment by the Super-Ego. Illness is employed as a means for this "self-punishment." The neurotic has to behave as though he were mastered by guilt, which the illness serves to punish, and so to relieve him.

QLA—ch. 5

The superego may bring fresh needs to the fore, but its chief function remains the *limitation* of satisfactions.

OoPA—ch. 2

See also *Ego and Its Relationship to the Superego; Repression.*

Superego and Its Relation to the Ego—The details of the relation between the ego and the superego become completely intelligible if they are carried back to the child's attitude toward his parents. The parents' influence naturally includes not merely the personalities of the parents themselves but also the racial, national, and family traditions handed on through them as well as the demands of the immediate social *milieu* which they represent. In the same way, an individual's superego in the course of his development takes over contributions from later successors and substitutes of his parents, such as teachers, admired figures in public life, or high social ideals. [Cf. also *Ego.*]   *OoPA—ch. 1*

Superego as Father-Substitute—The super-ego arises, as we know, from an identification with the father regarded as a model. Every such identification is in the nature of a desexualization or even of a sublimation.   *E & I—ch. 5*

Superego and Its Relation to the Id—In spite of their fundamental difference, the id and the superego have one thing in common: they both represent the influences of the past (the id the influence of heredity, the superego essentially the influence of what is taken over from other people), whereas the ego is principally determined by the individual's own experience, that is to say by accidental and current events.
OoPA—ch. 1

Superego and the Oedipus Complex—The superego is in fact the heir to the Œdipus complex and only arises after that complex has been disposed of.   *OoPA—ch. 8*

SUPERSTITION—The phenomena of superstition furnish another indication of the unconscious motivation in chance and faulty actions.   *PEL—ch. 10*

Because the superstitious person knows nothing of the motivation of his own accidental actions, and because the fact of this motivation strives for a place in his recognition, he is compelled to dispose of them by displacing them into the outer world. As a matter of fact, I believe that a large portion of the mythological conception of the world which reaches far into the most modern religions, *is nothing but psychology projected to the outer world.*   *PEL—ch. 10*

SYMPTOM—The symptom has its origin in the repressed, it is as it were the representative of the repressed in relation to the ego; the repressed is a foreign territory to the ego, an internal foreign territory, just as reality is—you must excuse the unusual expression—an external foreign territory.

NILP—ch. 3

[Cf. also *Inhibition and Symptom.*]

SYMPTOM AND CHANCE ACTION—Cases [of lapses of our motor function] in which the entire action appears rather inexpedient, I call "symptomatic and chance actions."

PEL—ch. 8

Symptom and the Ego—The process which through repression has become a symptom maintains its existence outside of the ego-organization and independent of it.

PoA—ch. 3

SYMPTOM-FORMATION—Symptoms result from the injuring of the instinctual impulse through repression.

PoA—ch. 2

Symptoms are supposed to be an indication of and substitute for an unachieved instinctual gratification; they are, that is, a result of a process of repression. *PoA—ch. 2*

Symptom formation thus has the actual result of putting an end to the danger situation. *PoA—ch. 9*

All phenomena of symptom-formation can be fairly described as "the return of the repressed." The disitnctive character of them, however, lies in the extensive distortion the returning elements have undergone, compared with their original form. *M & M—Part III, Section II*

See also *Compulsion Neurosis.*

SYPHILOPHOBIA—Castration anxiety persists in the guise of syphilophobia, after it has been learned that castration is no longer customary as a punishment for giving the sexual appetites free rein but that serious diseases threaten intinctual freedom instead. *PoA—ch. 9*

I may refer to the case of a young man who became agoraphobic because he was afraid of yielding to the allurements of prostitutes and of acquiring syphilis as a punishment.

PoA—ch. 7

SYSTEM—The secondary elaboration of the product of the dream-work is an excellent example of the nature and the pretensions of a system. An intellectual function in us demands the unification, coherence and comprehensibility of everything perceived and thought of, and does not hesitate to construct a false connection if, as a result of special circumstances, it cannot grasp the right one. We know such system formation not only from the dream, but also from phobias, from compulsive thinking and from the types of delusions. The system formation is most ingenious in delusional states (paranoia) and dominates the clinical picture, but it also must not be overlooked in other forms of neuropsychoses. In every case we can show that a rearrangement of the psychic material takes place, which may often be quite violent, provided it seems comprehensible from the point of view of the system. The best indication that a system has been formed then lies in the fact that each result of it can be shown to have at least two motivations, one of which springs from the assumptions of the system and is therefore eventually delusional—and a hidden one which, however, we must recognize as the real and effective motivation.   *T & T—ch. 3*

T

TABOO—Taboo is a Polynesian word, the translation of which provides difficulties for us because we no longer possess the idea which it connotes. It was still current with the ancient Romans: their word "sacer" was the same as the taboo of the Polynesians. The ἄγος of the Greeks and the Kodaush of the Hebrews must also have signified the same thing which the Polynesians express through their word taboo and what many races in America, Africa (Madagascar), North and Central Asia express through analogous designations.

For us the meaning of taboo branches off into two opposite directions. On the one hand it means to us, sacred, consecrated: but on the other hand it means, uncanny, dangerous, forbidden, and unclean. The oposite for taboo is designated in Polynesian by the word *noa* and signifies something accessible. Thus something like the concept of reserve inheres in taboo; taboo expresses itself essentially in prohibitions and restrictions. Our combination of "holy dread" would often express the meaning of taboo. *T & T—ch. 2*

Let us summarize what understanding we have gained of taboo through its comparison with the compulsive prohibition of the neurotic. Taboo is a very primitive prohibition imposed from without (by an authority) and directed against the strongest desires of man. The desire to violate it continues in the unconscious; persons who obey the taboo have an ambivalent feeling toward what is affected by the taboo. The magic power attributed to taboo goes back to its ability to lead man into temptation: it behaves like a contagion, because the example is contagious, and because the prohibited desire becomes displaced in the unconscious upon something else. The expiation for the violation of a taboo through a renunciation proves that a renunciation is at the basis of the observance of the taboo. *T & T—ch. 2*

Taboo and Compulsion Neurosis—He who approaches the problem of taboo from the field of psychoanalysis, which is concerned with the study of the unconscious part of the individual's psychic life, needs but a moment's reflection to realize that these phenomena are by no means foreign to him. He knows people who have individually created such taboo prohibitions for themselves, which they follow as strictly as savages observe the taboos common to their tribe or society. If he were not accustomed to call these individuals "compulsion neurotics" he would find the term "taboo disease" quite appropriate for their malady. Psychoanalytic investigation has taught him the clinical etiology and the essential part of the psychological mechanism of this compulsion disease, so that he cannot resist applying what he has learned there to explain corresponding manifestations in folk psychology.

There is one warning to which we shall have to give heed in making this attempt. The similarity between taboo and compulsion disease may be purely superficial, holding good only for the manifestations of both without extending into their deeper characteristics. . . . The first and most striking correspondence between the compulsion prohobitions of neurotics and taboo lies in the fact that the origin of these prohibitions is just as unmotivated and enigmatic. They have appeared at some time or other and must now be retained on account of an unconquerable anxiety. An external threat of punishment is superfluous, because an inner certainty (a conscience) exists that violation will be followed by unbearable disaster. The very most that compulsion patients can tell us is the vague premonition that some person of their environment will suffer harm if they should violate the prohibition. Of what the harm is to consist is not known, and this inadequate information is more likely to be obtained during the later discussions of the expiatory and defensive actions than when the prohibitions themselves are being discussed. . . . Compulsion prohibitions, like taboo prohibitions, entail the most extraordinary renunciations and restrictions of life, but a part of these can be removed by carrying out certain acts which now also must be done because they have acquired a compulsive character (obsessive acts); there is no doubt that these acts are in the nature of penances, expiations, defence reactions, and purifications. The most common of these obsessive acts is washing with water (washing obsession). A part of the taboo prohibitions can also be replaced in this way, that is to say, their violation can be made good through such a "ceremonial," and here too lustration through water is the preferred way.

Let us now summarize the points in which the correspondence between taboo customs and the symptoms of compulsion neurosis are most c'early manifested: 1. In the lack of motivation of the commandments, 2. in their enforcement through an inner need, 3. in their capacity for displacement and in the danger of contagion from what is prohibited, 4. and in the causation of ceremonial actions and commandments which emanate from the forbidden. *T & T—ch. 2*

Taboo and Touching—In its attempt to prevent associations from occurring, to obstruct the forming of connections in thought, the ego is complying with one of the oldest and most fundamental commandments of the compulsion neurosis, the taboo on touching. To the question why the avoidance of touching, contact or contagion plays so large a rôle in the neurosis and is made the content of so complicated a system, the answer is that touching, physical contact, is the most immediate aim of aggressive no less than of tender object-cathexes. Eros desires contact, for it strives for union, for the annihilation of spatial boundaries between ego and loved object. But destruction, too, which before the invention of long-range weapons could be effected only through proximity, necessarily presupposes physical contact, the use of the hands. To touch a woman has become in ordinary parlance a euphemism for her use as a sexual object. Not to touch the genital is the usual wording of the prohibition against auto-erotic gratification. Since the compulsion neurosis sought to effect erotic contact in the first place, and then, subsequent to regression, the same contact disguised as aggression, nothing was taboo to it in such intense degree as this very contact, nothing was so fitted to become the keystone of a system of prohibitions. *PoA—ch. 6*

TELEPATHY—You know that by telepathy we mean the alleged fact that an event which occurs at a specific time comes more or less simultaneously into the consciousness of a person who is spatially distant, without any of the known methods of communication coming into play. The tacit assumption is that this event occurs to a person, in whom the receiver of the message has some strong emotional interest. . . . I need not emphasize to you the improbability of such processes, and anyway there are good reasons for rejecting the majority of such reports. *NILP—ch. 2*

Have I given you the impression that I am secretly inclined to support the reality of telepathy in the occult sense? If so, I should very much regret that it is so difficult to avoid giving such an impression. In reality, however, I was anxious to be strictly impartial. I have every reason to be so, for I have no opinion; I know nothing about it.   *D & T*

Telepathy and Dream—Fundamentally the dream has but little to do with telepathy. Telepathy throws no new light on the nature of the dream, nor does the dream bear witness for the reality of telepathy. Telepathic phenomena are also by no manner of means confined to dreams; they can also manifest themselves during waking life. The only ground for mentioning the connection between dreams and telepathy is that the condition of sleep seems to be especially suitable for the reception of telepathic communications. If then one comes across a so-called telepathic dream, one can convince oneself by its analysis that the telepathic message has played the same rôle as any other residue of waking life, and as such has been altered by the dream-work and made to serve its purpose.

I want you to notice that it was not dreams that seemed to teach us something about telepathy, but the interpretation of the dreams, the psycho-analytic treatment of them.

NILP—ch. 2

THOUGHT-PROCESSES—Thought-processes, and what may be analogous to them in the Id, are unconscious *per se* and obtain their entry into consciousness by their connection, via the function of speech, with memory traces of perceptions through touch and ear.   *M & M—Part III, Section I*

THOUGHT-TRANSFERENCE—There is, for example, the phenomenon of thought-transference, which is closely allied to telepathy and, indeed, can be identified with it without much difficulty. It is held that psychological processes, ideas, states of excitement, volitions, which occur in the mind of one person, can be transferred through space to another, without the usual means of communication (words or signs) being employed. Incidentally it is remarkable that it is actually these phenomena which find the least mention in the old accounts of the miraculous.   *NILP—ch. 2*

TIME-PERCEPTION—The relation of time, too, which is so hard to describe, is communicated to the ego by the perceptual system; indeed it can hardly be doubted that the mode in which this system works is the source of the idea of time.

NILP—ch. 3

TOTEMISM—Among the Australians the system of *Totemism* takes the place of all religious and social institutions. Australian tribes are divided into small *septs* or clans, each taking the name of its *totem*. Now what is a totem? As a rule it is an animal, either edible or harmless, or dangerous and feared; more rarely the totem is a plant or a force of nature (rain, water), which stands in a peculiar relation to the whole clan. The totem is first of all the tribal ancestor of the clan, as well as its tutelary spirit and protector; it sends oracles and, though otherwise dangerous, the totem knows and spares its children. The members of a totem are therefore under a sacred obligation not to kill (destroy) their totem, to obstain from eating its meat or from any other enjoyment of it. Any violation of these prohibitions is automatically punished. The character of a totem is inherent not only in a single animal or a single being but in all the members of the species. From time to time festivals are held at which the members of a totem represent or imitate, in ceremonial dances, the movements and characteristics of their totems. . . . We must consider that peculiarity of the totemic system which attracts the interest of the psychoanalyst. Almost everywhere where the totem prevails, there also exists the law that *the members of the same totem are not allowed to enter into sexual relations with each other; that is, that they cannot marry each other*. This represents the *exogamy* which is associated with the totem.   *T & T—ch. 1*

Totemism as the Earliest Religion—Totemism, with its worship of a father substitute, the ambivalency towards the father which is evidenced by the totem feast, the institution of remembrance festivals and of laws the breaking of which is punished by death—this totemism, I conclude, may be regarded as the earliest appearance of religion in the history of mankind, and it illustrates the close connection existing from the very beginning of time between social institutions and moral obligations.   *M & M—Part III, Section I*

Though it may seem that instinctual renunciation, and the ethics based on it, do not belong to the essence of religion, still they are genetically closely related to religion. Totemism, the first form of religion of which we know, contains as an indispensable part of its system a number of laws and prohibitions which plainly mean nothing else but instinctual renunciation.

M & M—Part III, Section II

TOUCHING—To touch is the beginning of every act of possession, of every attempt to make use of a person or thing.

T & T—ch. 2

Touching, physical contact, is the most immediate aim of aggressive no less than of tender object-cathexes. [Cf. *Taboo on Touching.*]

PoA—ch. 6

TRADITION—Incomplete and dim memories of the past, which we call tradition, are a great incentive to the artist, for he is free to fill in the gaps in the memories according to the behests of his imagination and to form after his own purpose the image of the time he has undertaken to reproduce. One might almost say that the more shadowy tradition has become, the more meet is it for the poet's use.

M & M—Part III, Section I

TRANSFERENCE (IN ANALYSIS)—The patient sees in his analyst the return—the reincarnation—of some important figure out of his childhood or past, and consequently transfers on to him feelings and reactions that undoubtedly applied to this model. It soon becomes evident that this fact of transference is a factor of undreamed-of importance—on the one hand an instrument of irreplaceable value and on the other a source of serious dangers. This transference is *ambivalent:* it comprises positive and affectionate as well as negative and hostile attitudes toward the analyst, who, as a rule, is put in the place of one or other of the patient's parents, his father or his mother. So long as it is positive it serves us admirably. It alters the whole analytic situation and sidetracks the patient's rational aim of becoming well and free from his troubles. Instead of it there emerges the aim of pleasing the analyst, of winning his applause and his love. This becomes the true motive-force for the patient's collaboration; the weak ego becomes strong; under the influence of this aim the patient achieves things that would otherwise be beyond his power; his symptoms disappear and he seems to have recovered—all of this simply out of love for his analyst. . . . Therapeutic successes that take place under the sway of the positive transference are under the suspicion of being of a *suggestive* nature. If the negative transference gains the upper hand they are blown away like spray before the wind. [See also *Analyst, Personal Influence of.*]

OoPA—ch. 6

TRANSFERENCE OF THOUGHTS—See *Thought-Transference.*

TRANSFERENCE-LOVE—See *Transference in Analysis.*

TRAUMA (PSYCHIC)—In traumatic neurosis the active cause of illness is not the trifling bodily injury but the affect of fright—the psychic trauma. Similarly, our investigations of many, if not of the majority, of hysterical symptoms have revealed causes which must be described as psychic traumas.

PMHP—ch. 1

The impressions we experienced at an early age and forgot later, to which I have ascribed such great importance for the ætiology of the neuroses, are called traumata.

M & M—Part III, Section I

Trauma (Psychic), Fixation to the—Endeavors to revive the trauma, to remember the forgotten experience. . . . if it was an early affective relationship it is revived in an analogous connection with another person. . . . Thus a man who has spent his childhood in an excessive and since forgotten "mother-fixation," may all his life seek for a woman on whom he can be dependent, who will feed and keep him.

M & M—Part III, Section I

Trauma (Psychic) and the Formation of Neurosis—Our researches have shown that what we call the phenomena or symptoms of a neurosis are the consequences of certain experiences and impressions which, for this very reason, we recognize to be ætiological traumata. We wish to ascertain, even if only in a rough schematic way, the characteristics common to these experiences and to neurotic symptoms.

Let us first consider the former. All these traumata belong to early childhood, the period up to about five years. Impressions during the time when the child begins to speak are found to be especially interesting. The period between two and four years is the most important. How soon after birth this sensitiveness to traumata begins we are not able to state with any degree of certainty.

M & M—Part III, Section I

A trauma in childhood can be immediately followed by a neurosis during childhood; this constitutes an effort of defence accompanied by the formation of symptoms.

M & M—Part III, Section I

It may remain an open question whether the ætiology of the neurosis should in general be regarded as a traumatic one. The obvious objection is that a trauma is not always evident in the early history of the neurotic individual. Often we must be content to say that there is nothing else but an unusual reaction to experiences and demands that apply to all individuals; many people deal with them in another way which we may term normal. Where we can find no other explanation than a hereditary and constitutional disposition, we are naturally tempted to say that the neurosis was not suddenly acquired, but slowly developed.

In this connection, however, two points stand out. The first is that the genesis of the neurosis always goes back to very early impressions in childhood. The second is this: it is correct to say that there are cases which we single out as "traumatic" ones because the effects unmistakably go back to one or more strong impressions of this early period. They failed to be disposed of normally, so that one feels inclined to say that if this or that had not happened, there would have been no neurosis. It would be sufficient for our purposes even if we had to limit the analogy in question to the traumatic cases.

M & M—Part III, Section I

See also *Incubation Period of Traumatic Neuroses.*

TRAUMATIC FACTOR—See *Anxiety, Object of.*

TRAUMATIC NEUROSIS—See *Neurosis, Traumatic.*

TRUTH—See *Science.*

U

UCS.—Unconscious [*q.v.*]

UNCONSCIOUS—The oldest and best meaning of the word "unconscious" is the descriptive one; we call "unconscious" any mental process the existence of which we are obliged to assume—because, for instance, we infer it in some way from its effects—but of which we are not directly aware. . . . If we want to be more accurate, we should modify the statement by saying that we call a process "unconscious" when we have to assume that it was active *at a certain time,* although *at that time* we knew nothing about it.   *NILP—ch. 3*

Certainly, large portions of the ego and super-ego can remain unconscious, are, in fact, normally unconscious. That means to say that the individual knows nothing of their contents and that it requires an expenditure of effort to make him conscious of them. It is true, then, that ego and conscious, repressed and unconscious do not coincide.   *NILP—ch. 3*

Unconscious and Preconscious—There are *two kinds of unconscious,* which have not as yet been distinguished by psychologists. Both are unconscious in the psychological sense; but in our sense the first, which we call *Ucs.,* is likewise *incapable of consciousness;* whereas the second we call *Pcs.* because its excitations, after the observance of certain rules, are capable of reaching consciousness; perhaps not before they have again undergone censorship, but nevertheless regardless of the *Ucs. system.* The fact that in order to attain consciousness the excitations must pass through an unalterable series, a succession of instances, as is betrayed by the changes produced in them by the censorship, has enabled us to describe them by analogy in spatial terms. We described the relations of the two systems to each other and to consciousness by say-

161

ing that the system *Pcs.* is like a screen between the system *Ucs.* and consciousness. The system *Pcs.* not only bars access to consciousness, but also controls the access to voluntary motility, and has control of the emission of a mobile cathectic energy, a portion of which is familiar to us as attention.

IoD—ch. 7

UNCONSCIOUS MENTAL PROCESSES, TIMELESSNESS OF—We have found by experience that unconscious mental processes are in themselves "timeless." That is to say to begin with: they are not arranged chronologically, time alters nothing in them, nor can the idea of time be applied to them.

BPP—ch. 4

UNDOING—It is a kind of negative magic which by means of a motor symbolism would "blow away," as it were, not the consequences of an event (an impression, an experience), but the event itself. . . . The effort at "undoing" finds its reflection in the normal sphere in the resolve to treat an occurrence as *non arrivé;* but in this case one does not take up arms against it, one is simply not concerned about either the occurrence or its consequences; whereas in neurosis the attempt is made to abrogate the past itself, to repress it by motor means. An effort of the same sort may provide the explanation of the compulsion to *repetition* so frequently present in neurosis, a repetition in the carrying out of which various mutually contradictory purposes are commingled. . . . The striving to "undo" a traumatic experience is often revealed as a motive force of the first rank in the creating of symptoms.

PoA—ch. 6

UNPLEASURE—The ego's activities are governed by considerations of the tensions produced by stimuli present within it or introduced into it. The raising of these tensions is in general felt as *unpleasure* and their lowering as *pleasure.* [Cf. also *Anxiety, Signal of*.]   *OoPA—ch. 1*

The sensation of unpleasure which accompanies the appearance of symptoms varies to an extraordinary degree. In the case of the permanent symptoms where a displacement upon motility has occurred, such as paralyses and contractures, it is usually absent; the ego behaves towards them as if it were not involved; in the case of the intermittent symptoms and those in the sensory sphere, definite feelings of unpleasure are experienced as a rule, which may be increased to an excessive degree in the case of the symptom of pain. *PoA—ch. 5*

UTERUS, REGRESSION TO—See *Agoraphobia*.

V

VERBAL IMAGE—The part played by verbal images becomes perfectly clear. By their interposition internal thought-processes are made into perceptions.   *E & I—ch. 2*

VOMITING—As an hysterical defense against eating, the symptom of vomiting is familiar.   *PoA—ch. 1*

W

WALKING—Locomotion is inhibited in many neurotic states by antipathy to walking and weakness in walking: the hysterical disability makes use of paralysis of the motor apparatus or creates a specific suspension of this one function of the latter (abasia). Particularly characteristic are the difficulties of locomotion brought about by the interpolation of definite conditions as prerequisites, the non-fulfillment of which evokes anxiety (phobia). . . . If walking has become a symbolic substitute for stamping on the body of Mother Earth, then . . . walking will be abstained from, because it is as though forbidden sexual behavior were thereby indulged in.   *PoA—ch. 1*

WAR—Anything that encourages the growth of emotional ties between men must operate against war.   *WW*

WAR NEUROSIS—The war neuroses, in so far as they are distinguished from the ordinary neuroses of peace-time by special characteristics, are to be regarded as traumatic neuroses whose occurrence has been made possible or has been promoted by a conflict in the ego.   *PAWN*

WEANING—It is probable that the fear of poisoning is connected with weaning. Poison is the nourishment that makes one ill. Perhaps, moreover, the child traces his early illnesses back to this frustration. [Cf. also *Milk*.]   *NILP—ch. 5*

WELTANSCHAUUNG—*"Weltanschauung"* is, I am afraid, a specifically German notion, which it would be difficult to translate into a foreign language. If I attempt to give you a definition of the word, it can hardly fail to strike you as inept. By *Weltanschauung*, then, I mean an intellectual construction, which gives a unified solution of all the problems of our existence in virtue of a comprehensive hypothesis, a construction, therefore, in which no question is left open and in which everything in which we are interested finds a place. It is easy to see that the possession of such a *Weltanshchauung* is one of the ideal wishes of mankind. When one believes in such a thing, one feels secure in life, one knows what one ought to strive after, and how one ought to organise one's emotions and interests to the best purpose.   *NILP—ch. 7*

WISH-FULFILMENT (IN DREAMS)—We assert that the dream is a wish-fulfilment; in order to take objections into account, you may say that the dream is an *attempted* wish-fulfilment. [See also *Dream and Wish-Fulfilment*.]
                                                   NILP—ch. 1

WIT—Wit is, so to speak, the contribution to the comic from the sphere of the unconscious.   *WRU—ch. VII*

Though wit-making is an excellent means of obtaining pleasure from the psychic processes, we know that not all persons are equally able to make use of it. Wit-making is not at the disposal of all, in general there are but a few persons to whom one can point and say that they are witty. Here wit seems to be a special ability somewhere within the region of the old "psychic faculties," and this shows itself in its appearance as fairly independent of the other faculties such as intelligence, phantasy, memory, etc. A special talent or psychic determination permitting or favoring wit-making must be presupposed in all wit-makers.   *WRU—ch. V*

It has seemed to us that the pleasure of wit originates from an *economy of expenditure in inhibition,* of the comic from an *economy of expenditure in thought,* and of humor from an *economy of expenditure in feeling.* All three modes of activity of our psychic apparatus derive pleasure from economy. All three present methods strive to bring back from the psychic activity a pleasure which has really been lost in the development of this activity. For the euphoria which we are thus striving to obtain is nothing but the state of a bygone time, in which we were wont to defray our phychic work with slight expenditure. It is the state of our childhood in which we did not know the comic, were incapable of wit, and did not need humor to make us happy.   *WRU—ch. VII*

Wit and Dream—The most important difference lies in their social behavior. The dream is a perfectly asocial psychic product. It has nothing to tell to anyone else, having originated in an individual as a compromise between conflicting psychic forces it remains incomprehensible to the person himself and has therefore altogether no interest for anybody else. Not only does the dream find it unnecessary to place any value on intelligibleness, but it must even guard against being understood, as it would then be destroyed; it can only exist in disguised form. For this reason the dream may make use freely of the mechanism that controls unconscious thought processes to the extent of producing undecipherable distortions. Wit, on the other hand, is the most social of all those psychic functions whose aim is to gain pleasure. It often requires three persons, and the psychic process which it incites always requires the participation of at least one other person. It must therefore bind itself to the condition of intelligibleness; it may employ distortion made practicable in the unconscious through condensation and displacement, to no greater extent than can be deciphered by the intelligence of the third person. As for the rest, wit and dreams have developed in altogether different spheres of the psychic life, and are to be classed under widely separated categories of the psychological system. No matter how concealed, the dream is still a wish, while wit is a developed play. Despite its apparent unreality, the dream retains its relation to the great interests of life; it seeks to supply what is lacking through a regressive detour of hallucinations; and it owes its existence solely to the strong need for sleep during the night. Wit, on the other hand, seeks to draw a small amount of pleasure from the free and unencumbered activities of our psychic apparatus, and later to seize this pleasure as an incidental gain. It thus *secondarily* reaches to important functions relative to the outer world. The dream serves preponderantly to guard against pain, while wit serves to acquire pleasure; in these two aims all our psychic activities meet.

WRU—ch. VI

As we know that displacements in dream-work point to the influence of censorship of conscious thought, we will consequently be inclined to assume that an inhibiting force also plays a part in the formation of wit when we find the process of displacement among the techniques of wit. We also know that this is commonly the case; the endeavor of wit to revive the old pleasure in nonsense or the old pleasure in word-play meets with resistance in every normal state, a resistance which is exerted by the protest of critical reason, and which must be overcome in each individual case. But a radical distinction between wit and dreams is shown in the manner in which the witwork solves this difficulty. In the dream-work the solution of this task is brought about regularly through displacements and through the choice of ideas which are remote enough from those objectionable to secure passage through the censorship; the latter themselves are but offsprings of those whose psychic cathexis they have taken over through full transference. The displacements are, therefore, not lacking in any dream and are far more compresensive. They not only include the deviations from the trend of thought, but also all forms of indirect expression, especially the substitution for an important but offensive element by one indifferent and seemingly harmless to the censorship, which then looks like a most remote allusion to the first; they also include substitution through symbols, comparisons, or trifies. It is not to be denied that parts of this indirect representation really originate in the foreconscious thoughts of the dream—as, for example, symbolical representation and representation through comparisons—because otherwise the thought would not have reached the state of the foreconscious expression. Such indirect expressions and allusions, whose reference to the original thought is easily detectable, are really permissible and customary means of expression even in our conscious thought. The dream-work, however, exaggerates the application of these means of indirect expression to an unlimited degree. Under the pressure of the censor any kind of association becomes good enough for substitution by allusion; the displacement from one element to any other is permitted. The substitution of the inner associations (similarity, causal connection, etc.) by the so-called outer associations (simultaneity, contiguity in space, assonance) is particularly conspicuous and characteristic of the dream-work.   *WRU—ch. VI*

Wit and Dream-Work—Absurdity in wit frequently stands for derision and criticism in the thought behind the witticism, wherein the wit-work follows the dream-work.
                                            WRU—ch. III

WOMAN—. . . . the female sex, the sex certainly more predisposed to neurosis. . . . It is precisely in the female that object loss seems to remain the most effective situation of danger. . . . Since it is certainly true that hysteria has a greater affinity with femininity, just as compulsion neurosis has with masculinity, the idea suggests itself that, as a determinant of anxiety, loss of love plays a rôle in hysteria similar to that of the threat of castration in the phobias and of dread of the superego in compulsion neurosis. *PoA—ch. 8*

We attribute to women a greater amount of narcissism (and this influences their object-choice) so that for them to be loved is a stronger need than to love. Their vanity is partly a further effect of penis-envy, for they are driven to rate their physical charms more highly as a belated compensation for their original sexual inferiority. Modesty, which is regarded as a feminine characteristic *par excellence,* but is far more a matter of convention than one would think, was, in our opinion, originally designed to hide the deficiency in her genitals. *NILP—ch. 5*

[Cf. also *Child, Girl; Parents (Mother); Penis-Envy; Sexuality, Female.*]

WORDS [cf. also SPEECH; VERBAL IMAGE]—We do not, indeed, wish to decry *words*. They are a mighty instrument, the means by which we convey our feelings, the way by which we influence others. Words can do unutterable good, and appalling harm. No doubt, in the beginning was the deed—the word came later; in some contexts it was a cultural advance when deeds were moderated to words. But still, words were originally spells, acts of magic, and they still retain much of their old power. *QLA—ch. 1*

WORK—The great majority work only when forced by necessity, and this natural human aversion to work gives rise to the most difficult social problems. *C & D—ch. 2*

WORKING-OVER—We know that the anxiety of the neuroses can be relieved by further mental "working-over," *e.g.* by conversion, reaction-formation or defence-formation (phobia). *Narc*

WORKING-THROUGH PERIOD—[See also *Ego-Resistance.*]

WRITING—If writing—which consists in allowing a fluid to flow out from a tube upon a piece of white paper—has acquired the symbolic meaning of coitus . . . then writing will be abstained from, because it is as though forbidden sexual behavior were thereby being indulged in. *PoA—ch. 1*

Z

ZOOPHOBIA, INFANTILE—The relation of the child to animals has much in common with that of primitive man. The child does not yet show any trace of the pride which afterwards moves the adult civilized man to set a sharp dividing line between his own nature and that of all other animals. The child unhesitatingly attributes full equality to animals; he probably feels himself more closely related to the animal than to the undoubtedly mysterious adult, in the freedom with which he acknowledges his needs.

Not infrequently a curious disturbance manifests itself in this excellent understanding between child and animal. The child suddenly begins to fear a certain animal species and to protect himself against seeing or touching any individual of this species. There results the clinical picture of an *animal phobia*, which is one of the most frequent among the psychoneurotic diseases of this age and perhaps the earliest form of such an ailment. The phobia is as a rule in regard to animals for which the child has until then shown the liveliest interest and has nothing to do with the individual animal. In cities the choice of animals which can become the object of phobia is not great. They are horses, dogs, cats, more seldom birds, and strikingly often very small animals like bugs and butterflies. Sometimes animals which are known to the child only from picture books and fairy stories become objects of the senseless and inordinate anxiety which is manifested with these phobias; it is seldom possible to learn the manner in which such an unusual choice of anxiety has been brought about. I am indebted to Dr. Karl Abraham for the report of a case in which the child itself explained its fear of wasps by saying that the colour and the stripes of the body of the wasp had made it think of the tiger of which, from all that it had heard, it might well be afraid.

The animal phobias have not yet been made the object of

careful analytical investigation, although they very much merit it. The difficulties of analyzing children of so tender an age have probably been the motive of such neglect. It cannot therefore be asserted that the general meaning of these illnesses is known, and I myself do not think that it would turn out to be the same in all cases. But a number of such phobias directed against larger animals have proved accessible to analysis and have thus betrayed their secret to the investigator. In every case it was the same: the fear at bottom was of the father, if the children examined were boys, and was merely displaced upon the animal.   *T & T—ch. 4*

In infantile zoöphobias, the ego must intervene against a libidinal object-cathexis of the id (that of the positive or negative œdipus complex, namely), because of the recognition that to yield to it would entail the danger of castration. . . . The castration anxiety is given another object and a distorted expression—namely, that of being bitten by a horse (or eaten by a wolf) instead of being castrated by the father. . . . The anxiety in zoöphobia is thus an affective reaction of the ego to danger, the danger which is in this case warned against being that of castration.   *PoA—ch. 7*

Key to References *

(ch. — chapter)

ABS—An Autobiographical Study.

A-N—The Justification for Detaching from Neurasthenia a Particular Syndrome: The Anxiety-Neurosis. (Collected Papers, Vol. 1)

AnDS—Some Psychological Consequences of the Anatomical Distinction between the Sexes. (Collected Papers, Vol. V)

APF—The Acquisition of Power over Fire. (Collected Papers, Vol. V)

AP5B—Analysis of a Phobia in a Five-Year-Old Boy. (Collected Papers, Vol. III)

ASPW—The Antithetical Sense of Primal Words. (Collected Papers, Vol. IV)

AT & I—Analysis, Terminable and Interminable. (Collected Papers, Vol. V)

BPP—Beyond the Pleasure Principle.

C & AE—Character and Anal Erotism. (Collected Papers, Vol. II)

C & D—Civilization and Its Discontents.

CPL-DEL—Contributions to the Psychology of Love. The Most Prevalent Form of Degradation in Erotic Life. (Collected Papers, Vol. IV)

CPL-TV—Contributions to the Psychology of Love. The Taboo of Virginity. (Collected Papers, Vol. IV)

C-S&E—A Connection between a Symbol and a Symptom. (Collected Papers, Vol. II)

CSMN—"Civilized" Sexual Morality and Modern Nervousness. (Collected Papers, Vol. II)

CSOHP—Some points in a Comparative Study of Organic and Hysterical Paralysis. (Collected Papers, Vol. I)

---

* For the names of publishers and copyright-owners, see "Acknowledgment," on page 176.

DNP—The Defence of Neuro-Psychoses. (Collected Papers, Vol. I)

D & T—Dreams and Telepathy. (Collected Papers, Vol. IV)

E & I—The Ego and the Id.

EPM—The Economic Problem in Masochism. (Collected Papers, Vol. II)

Fet—Fetishism. (Collected Papers, Vol. V)

FPMF—Formulations regarding the two Principles in Mental Functioning. (Collected Papers, Vol. IV)

FPT—The Future Prospects of Psycho-Analytic Therapy. (Collected Papers, Vol. II)

FRDNP—Further Remarks on the Defence Psycho-Neuroses. (Collected Papers, Vol. I)

FS—Female Sexuality. (Collected Papers, Vol. V)

GPAE—Group Psychology and the Analysis of the Ego.

GRHA—General Remarks on Hysterical Attacks. (Collected Papers, Vol. II)

HAN—Heredity and the Aetiology of the Neuroses. (Collected Papers, Vol. 1)

HIF—From the History of an Infantile Neurosis. (Collected Papers, Vol. III)

H & S—Hypnotism and Suggestion. (Collected Papers, Vol. V)

Hum—Humour. (Collected Papers, Vol. V)

IoD—The Interpretation of Dreams.

I & V—Instincts and their Vicissitudes. (Collected Papers, Vol. IV)

IML—Infantile Mental Life. (Collected Papers, Vol. 1)

LDV—Leonardo da Vinci.

LT—The Libido Theory. (Collected Papers, Vol. V)

M & M—Moses and Monotheism.

MSTD—Metapsychological Supplement to the Theory of Dreams. (Collected Papers, Vol. IV)

Narc—On Narcissism: an Introduction. (Collected Papers, Vol. IV)

Neg—Negation. (Collected Papers, Vol. V)

NILP—New Introductory Lectures on Psychoanalysis.

NM-JPH—Certain Neurotic Mechanisms in Jealousy. Paranoia and Homosexuality. (Collected Papers, Vol. II)

N & P—Neurosis and Psychosis. (Collected Papers, Vol. II)

OA & RL—Obsessive Acts and Religious Practices. (Collected Papers, Vol. II)

OoPA—An Outline of Psychoanalysis.

O & P—Obsessions and Phobias; their Psychical Mechanisms and their Aetiology. (Collected Papers, Vol. I)

OSD—The Occult Significance of Dreams. (Collected Papers, Vol. V)

PA—Psycho-Analysis. (Collected Papers, Vol. V)

PA & CL—Psycho-Analysis and the Ascertaining of Truth in Courts of Law. (Collected Papers, Vol. II)

ParDP—Psycho-Analytic Notes upon an Autobiographical Account of a Case of Paranoia (Dementia Paranoides). Collected Papers, Vol. III)

PEL—Psychopathology of Everyday Life.

PMHP—On the Psychical Mechanism of Hysterical Phenomena. (Collected Papers, Vol. I)

PoA—The Problem of Anxiety.

PON—The Predisposition to Obsessional Neurosis. Collected Papers, Vol. II)

PT—On Psychotherapy. (Collected Papers, Vol. I)

PVD—Psychogenic Visual Disturbance according to Psycho-Analytical Conceptions. (Collected Papers, Vol. II)

QLA—The Question of Lay Analysis.

RCA-N—A reply to Criticisms on the Anxiety-Neurosis. (Collected Papers, Vol. I)

Repr—Repression. (Collected Papers, Vol. IV)

RPDD—The Relation of the Poet to Day-Dreaming. (Collected Papers, Vol. IV)

SAoN—Sexuality in the Aetiology of Neuroses. (Collected Papers, Vol. I)

SECh—The Sexual Enlightenment of Children. (Collected Papers, Vol. II)

SM—Screen Memories. (Collected Papers, Vol. V)

TCTS—Three Contributions to the Theory of Sex.

THA—On the Theaory of Hysterical Attacks. (Collected Papers, Vol. V)

TIAE—On the Transformation of Instincts with Special Reference to Anal Erotism. (Collected Papers, Vol. II)

TNN—Types of Neurotic Nosogenesis. (Collected Papers, Vol. II)

TPDI—Remarks upon the Theory and Practice of Dream-Interpretation. (Collected Papers, Vol. V)

T & T—Totem and Taboo.

TTWD—Thoughts for the Times on War and Death. (Collected Papers, Vol. IV)

Uncanny—The "Uncanny". (Collected Papers, Vol. IV)

Ucs—The Unconscious. Collected Papers, Vol. IV)

WRU—Wit and Its Relation to the Unconscious.

WW—Why War? (Collected Papers, Vol. V)

Acknowledgments

The editors and the publisher of the present volume take this opportunity to express their grateful acknowledgment and thanks to the publishers and owners of copyrights listed below for their kind permission to quote copyrighted material from the following books and papers by Dr. Sigmund Freud:

George Allen & Unwin Ltd., London, England, publisher of *The Interpretation of Dreams.*

Ernest Benn Ltd., London, England, publisher of *Psychopathology of Everyday Life.*

Mrs. A. A. Brill, New York, N. Y., owner of copyright of *Totem and Taboo* and *Wit and Its Relation to the Unconscious.*

Dodd, Mead & Co., New York, N. Y., American publisher of *Totem and Taboo* and *Wit and Its Relation to the Unconscious.*

The Hogarth Press Ltd., London, England, publisher of *An Autobiographical Study, Civilization and Its Discontents, Collected Papers (Vols. I-V), Beyond the Pleasure Principle, The Ego and the Id, Group Psychology and the Analysis of the Ego.*

Alfred Knopf, Inc., New York, N. Y., publisher of *Moses and Monotheism.*

Nervous and Mental Disease Monographs, New York, N. Y., publisher of *Three Contributions to the Theory of Sex.*

W. W. Norton & Co., Inc., New York, N. Y., publisher of *New Introductory Lectures on Psychoanalysis, An Outline of Psychoanalysis, The Problem of Anxiety, The Question of Lay Analysis* (quotations by permission of W. W. Norton & Co., Inc., copyright, 1933, by Sigmund Freud, 1936, by The Psychoanalytical Quarterly, Inc., 1949, 1950, by W. W. Norton & Co., Inc.).

Random House, Inc., New York, N. Y., publisher of *Leonardo da Vinci—A Study in Psychosexuality* and *The Basic Writings of Sigmund Freud.*

Routledge & Kegan Paul Ltd., London, England, British publisher of *Totem and Taboo* and *Wit and Its Relation to the Unconscious.*